And
Grace Will
Lead Me
Home

And Grace Will Lead Me Home

A Spiritual Journey

JOHN POWERS

Foreword by
ANDREW GREELEY

ROMAN CATHOLIC CHURCH
JESUS CENTERED & PURPOSE DRIVEN

10851 Ridge Road
Seminole, Florida 33778

McCracken Press

New York

McCracken Press™
An imprint of Multi Media Communicators, Inc.
575 Madison Avenue, Suite 1006
New York, NY 10022

Cover art by Tim Ladwig
Cover design by Jim Hellman

Library of Congress Cataloging-in-Publication Data:
Powers, John D.
    And grace will lead me home: a spiritual journey /
John Powers: foreword by Andrew Greeley. — 1st ed.
      p.   cm.
    Includes bibliographical references.
    ISBN 1-56977-635-0: $9.95
    1. Spiritual life.   I. Title.
BV4501.2.P599 1994   94-31498
248—dc20   CIP

10 9 8 7 6 5 4 3 2 1

First Edition

Printed in the United States of America

Dedication

To Tom and Mary Powers, who
started my story spinning.

Thanks

Stephen Scharper, Katie and Timothy Conrod,
Carl Lorentzen, Mark Dupont, Tom Pollard,
Terry Kristofak, Joe Sedley, Kevin Sousa,
Eileen Fucito, Bill Walsh, Rich Broggini,
Rick Frechette, Francis Roberge,
Eugene Bonacci, Donna Camera,
Vincent Youngberg, Bonaventure Moccia,
Bob Joerger, Joseph Girzone, Andrew Greeley,
and members of the Hartford Readers Group.

FOREWORD

There is much talk about story telling within the priesthood today, as the clergy catch up on what they take to be the latest academic theological fashion. However, neither pastoral clergy nor academic theologians devote much of their time to telling stories, save perhaps for the personal anecdote to seize the attention of the congregation before beginning the prosaic part of the homily (a practice which Jesus did not follow, by the way). Such anecdotes have little value as stories because they lack the structure a true narrative should have and the enchanting element of surprise which must mark the end of every effective story (and hence the personal anecdote must be carefully planned if it is to become a narrative.

But allegorical stories are rare as hens' teeth (I almost said as rare as a brave bishop). While much of the interpretation of the Scripture through the centuries has been allegorical, the allegory as a story form seems to have slipped into disgrace as a result perhaps of the emergence of modern biblical exegesis.

So Father Powers skates on thin ice when he tries to write an allegory (in which allusions to Bunyan abound). Moreover he takes extra chances when his allegory is actually a memoir, an account of a life "in progress."

That he carries it off so well is a tribute to his skills and energy as a storyteller.

I found myself wondering while I read it whether the allegorical autobiography is more transparent than the ordinary memoir. Does the allegorical biographer make himself more vulnerable than the standard autobiographer? Is the allegory a way to hide or a way to reveal?

I concluded that it is both: Some parts of the self are less apparent in the allegory but other parts are more apparent. Neither style is better than the other. Both have legitimate uses. The author muse makes his choices to fit his tastes and goals.

Father Powers could well defend his choice on the ground that this is the way Grace has led him.

The reader should beware: Grace lurks everywhere. She lurks in this story and, if you don't watch out, She'll get you.

Andrew Greeley
Memorial Day 1994

CONTENTS

PREFACE

In forty-something years I have learned that the only good reason to look backward is to move forward while at the same time trying to add something positive to the world around me.

Memory, however, has a unique way of transforming what is remembered. Not only is memory selectively half blind but it is also oddly retroactive. Memory rewrites as much as it recollects, reshaping stories, myths, personal parables and tales as it recalls experience. Because memory is thirty to fifty percent imagination, it can't help but fictionalize the spaces between the facts, reconstructing what is remembered into an as yet unfinished story.

Autobiographical storytelling, therefore, not only helps to discipline the memory but it can also help uncover the heart's deepest desires, dreams and destiny while all the while reweaving the human psyche and spirit.

This book is an allegory of fictionalized fact, a psycho-spiritual autobiography. It is my story, fictionalized. I spin this tale not for pity or applause, however, but rather to follow an insightful recommendation by the noted scholar of mythology, Joseph Campbell, when in response to a question put to him by Bill Moyers in a television interview, replied:

"Preachers err by trying to talk people into belief, better they reveal the radiance of their own discoveries."[1]

I begin the telling of my tale with the assumption that my story is, in some measure, everyone's story. It's a story about a journey, traveled on the roads of tragedy, comedy, romance and irony. It's the heroic journey every human being is required to make, one way or the other.

And
Grace Will
Lead Me
Home

CELESTIAL CLASS 90249

Once upon a time, or to be more precise, long before I had even an inkling of an idea as to what time was, I sat comfortably in the fetal position in the back row of Celestial lecture room 90249. There, along with the estimated 271,232 other pre-borns expecting to be born in the world that day, I waited for what I was told would be a most painful event.

Attending the nine months of life preparation classes was a prerequisite for birth. Every day I sat with my classmates listening to the firmly sincere yet soothing voice of the divine mentor we knew only as Grace. Her affirming presence not only gifted us with all that was necessary to live at home with ourselves and each other in the before-life, but Grace also prepared us for the inevitable life to come.

Grace was the passionate heart of God, beating in our hearts, the glue of the universe, the beneficial influence of God, a terrible beauty, a savage gift, a golden mulatto-skinned woman elegantly and eternally moving and mentoring through the universe of mind, spirit, space, nature, emotions, and imagination. She was then and is today the mighty mystery that keeps every life traveler personally connected not only to one another but to God.

I don't want to give the impression here that I was the most industrious of students in the course on life preparation, because I wasn't. Even then, I found myself easily distracted by the pre-borns around me.

Sitting far in the back of the huge lecture room made it especially easy to converse with the girl sitting fetally to my right. We talked often about our life expectations and dreams. When I asked, for example, in what part of the world she wanted to be born, she responded without hesitation that she was not so concerned with where she would be born but rather hoped only to be born into a loving family. I too wanted to be born into love but I also held a hidden desire to be born in a place called Florida.

Although no one had ever returned to the womb to tell us what life was like after birth I had heard rumors that Florida was a warm and bright place. I was ready for bright.

In the middle of my conversation with the attractive pre-born next to me, Grace suddenly called out sternly:

"The two of you chatting back there, pay attention. If you, John," Grace continued, as she marched up the aisle in my direction, "are so easily distracted here in life-preparation class, I can just imagine how divided within yourself you'll become once you're born. Perhaps we should keep you for a few more days, just to make sure you've learned how to listen.

"Don't you realize," Grace asked, as she finally came to a halt directly in front of my desk, "that life is about paying attention? When you're born, John, it won't be so easy to hear my voice. I won't be so obvious.

"From being one person, a centered 'I,' knitted together in heart and soul with the heart and soul of God you will become a scattered 'we,' divided in mind, body, emotions, and needs, all fighting for control and attention.

"Oh, you will desperately long to be at home again with yourself, to be an 'I' that listens to the deep voice that resonates in heart and soul, but emotions, brain-chatter, and the need to please others will divide your loyalty, battling to dominate your identity, dividing you into a 'we.'

"Once you become a 'we,' John, you will, like so many others, frantically look to situations, people or transitory ideas and feelings to make you happy, forgetting that happiness was at home in you all along. Please, John, pay attention," Grace concluded.

Suddenly I felt what Grace had earlier described as a contraction begin to pull me away from the sound of her voice and the company of my classmates. I turned my attention to Grace's face and stared intently. I wanted to remember what she looked like; those eyes, that subtle and shadowed face.

As the contractions grew more frequent I drew further away, squinting my eyes to hold Grace in focus while straining to hear her tell me again how messy birth would be, how hard it would be to breathe for a few minutes (although I still didn't know what a minute was), and how cold it would be until someone took me in their arms.

With every pull and push I moved closer and closer to the birth canal, eventually losing sight of Grace altogether. I could barely hear the echo of her voice as she recited again some of the lessons she had struggled for months to drone into my soft skull. She said:

"Remember, God gives what God is, to all, all the time, in equal measure: the creativity to make life out of love and loss, the courage to rise again when you fall or fail, the compassion to do what you can, where you are, with what you've got and to even try the impossible, the capacity to contemplate the reality of God as you are being contemplated, and finally to enjoy the making of your own heart and soul out of the absurd bits and pieces of life. God gives what God is, do the same and die trying.

"Life, after all," Grace continued, "may not give you the kind of happenings and happiness you want, but it will give you what you need most—the graceful gifts of creativity, courage, compassion, contemplative presence, and humor to make life out of what happens."

A shudder coursed through my stretching frame as I was suddenly touched by a large human hand. Trying not to let the intrusion distract me from Grace's teachings, I turned my heart to her reflective whisperings.

"Reality," Grace said, "is like a sea you're thrown into without choice. Since you can't forever fight the currents or flee to dry safety, flow, swimming with the tide, face upward toward the sun.

"Remember," Grace continued, "that the universe is chaos huddled together, at home with itself. It was not, however, constructed for your personal pleasure and comfort. Enjoy all that makes life. Pain may be the inevitable result of life consisting of change, but misery does not have to be your only option.

"Recall too," she said, "that the universe, Earth, every gas and molecule, person and creature is a flaring forth of the Creator. Live at one with all that shares your source.

"And please, John, do all you can to remember that it is perspective, how you look at and live with yourself that will determine 99.9 percent of the time how you will look at and live with others, the world, and God.

"Since all learning is remembering," Grace continued, "I beg you to look for me in life. While I may seem, at times, hidden behind happenings, I promise to be an eternal presence, a seductive and inevitable Grace that will lead you home."

Just as someone grabbed hold of my head and pulled, I heard Grace speak her final message in a whisper as soft as dust. She said,

"John, look for me in the eyes of the grace-bearers that will move in and out of your life: Paul Joseph, the brother you will come to love but will lose to death; Aquinas, an elder monk, who will teach you about passion; the Artist of Psyche, or the mentoring psychotherapist who will guide you into yourself; Richard, the Missionary, your companion in the Valley of Poverty; and Santos, a holy child, who will set you free with a touch.

"Wherever you are, John, I will be at the heart of the matter leading you home to yourself. I will be there in your love and loss, pain and grief, failure and burnout, therapy and prayer, laughter and tears. We eternal travelers travel best, after all, when we travel together."

ISLAND OF IGNORANCE

What my young friend from lecture room 90249 had hoped for herself I had received: birth into a nurturing family. I was held and touched, protected and sheltered, sung to and rocked by parents who did what they thought, and had been taught, was most caring.

Like all other humans, I too was born onto the Island of Ignorance, destined to spend the rest of my life trying to remember and learn what it is to live at home with myself, others, and God amid the change and pain of life.

Naked I may have come into the world but naked I did not remain for long, for on the Island of Ignorance socialization clothed my personality with the suit of proper functioning, fitting me in the acceptable colors of behavior and beliefs. I learned quickly to measure up to the expected standards for a white male child in American society.

While I learned on the Island to idolize external authority, I also learned to trivialize internal realities. I may have learned how to function correctly in the outer world but I remained ignorant of the inner world of emotions, fantasies, desires, and dreams.

I learned how to fit in, pretending to be at home in the world of social convention, easily forgetting what Grace had taught—that ultimately happiness means being at home with yourself.

For almost ten years I wandered aimlessly along the shores of the Island of Ignorance, unaware that I'd become deaf to the whisperings of Grace in the worlds around and within me.

No longer could I hear her rhythm in nature, see her face behind all others, or feel the flow of her presence in my veins. I'd become a victim of the plagues that infected the Island: collective amnesia and denial.

No longer did I long for the happiness of oneness with myself, the Earth, others, and Grace. Instead I became disconnected and lonely, and like so many others, addicted to the illusions that society proclaimed would make me happy: pleasure, power, position, prestige, and pennies, billions of pennies, all awaiting me, I was told, just across the bay in the Land of Fantasy.

Day and night I paced unreflectively on the beach of the Island staring across the Sea of Reality at the Land of Fantasy, where the quick fixes of feeling good, success, control, dominance, and goodies were piled high for the taking, or so went the story of a society that also had become deaf to the murmurings of Grace.

I learned quickly that on the Island of Ignorance and in the Land of Fantasy it is not authenticity that is valued but conformity, not honest content of emotion that is respected but rather pleasing and eye-catching appearance.

I learned very early in my docile life that it was more important to make believe that I was perfectly without flaw than it was to believe in myself. In no uncertain terms the social atmosphere in which I was nurtured expected me to feign happiness while hiding all brokenness and pain, and if, God forbid, I discovered I was essentially flawed, I should keep such knowledge secret so as not to threaten the fortresslike walls of illusion I and others had built so high.

Getting a fleeting fix of pleasure was easy. All I had to do was allow society to write and authorize my life story by pleasing others for acceptance' sake, by coloring only inside the lines of proper behavior. Of course, I wanted to be happy and since happiness was, I was told, getting what I wanted, I tried to fit into a society that promised me all, and perhaps even more than I deserved, if I would only keep secret any emotions or thoughts that might disturb the comfort or conscience of my neighbors on Ignorance Island.

Although I'd forgotten Grace's promise to be with me always, I still knew deep in my nature that Grace was a force as persistent and inescapable as gravity. I would open my heart to her again and again in the flow of the next thirty-five years of life.

WAVE OF LOVE AND LOSS

Early one morning, as I was combing the beach along the far shore of the Isle of Ignorance for any bits of pleasure that might have washed up from the Land of Fantasy, I was suddenly knocked off my feet by a huge Wave of Love and Loss. The swell was so strong that as it washed over me it dragged my body and soul along with it into the rough waters of experience.

I must confess that I did not want to leave the blissful Island I'd grown so accustomed to. Ignorance was the only home I could remember and I would not risk losing it without a struggle. I tried to dig my fingers into the sand for security but the force of love pulled me out into the Sea of Reality where I swam, following the shifting currents.

The wave of experience that swept me off the Island of Ignorance was the real-life birth of my brother Paul Joseph. Paul was the seventh child born into a family in which I, at age nine, was the second oldest. Paul, however, was born with a rare heart disease that would take his life in only four years.

I do not recall, at this point of my drifting, how I knew Paul was dying of a terminal disease, but I knew. Whether my mother or father had told my brothers and sisters and me or whether one by one we were able to fit the pieces of extended hospital stays, adult whisperings, and medication bottles into the puzzle of knowledge I do not recall. Knowing the fact that Paul was dying, though, and being aware of how I felt about it were two different things.

Since death was a stranger to me, visiting others but not my family, the knowledge that Paul was dying did not slip easily into belief. My parents had done their jobs well protecting us from the harsh realities of life but they could not hide us from the worst of life's pains, the agony of watching a loved one suffer.

Until I lived with my brother Paul, pain had not yet been a significant part of the package of life for me. Neither had falling in love. While living on the Island of Ignorance, however, I had learned to do one thing well, to deny the reality of how I felt.

As is often the case in a family of seven children, it is commonly necessary for survival that both parents work. In fact, I can recall my father, at one point, having three jobs just to make those notorious ends everyone likes to talk about even come close to meeting.

I'm sure Paul's illness was far more emotionally and financially difficult for my mother and father than I could appreciate at the time, but they did what they were taught, worked triply hard while suffering in silence. As my parents had learned so they taught by example. What pain was felt was endured. With mounting hospital bills, seven small mouths to feed and souls to awaken there was little for anyone to do but what little they could to ease the family pain.

What I could do, it seemed, was help my parents take care of Paul. I became both by selection and choice one of Paul's primary caregivers. I'm confident that my brothers and sisters shared a profound love for Paul but my memory has stored only the bits of information that reveal my growing attachment to this frail child of life.

I was awakened to loving Paul as I nurtured him. Through the feedings, diaper changes, and hospital visits I sank more deeply in love with him. While my parents worked in the late evenings, round and round in the darkness of the first floor of our home I walked with Paul in my arms, soothing him through his pain. By whispering what stories I knew or could make up and by humming deeply so that my chest would vibrate against his ear, I helped Paul find a friend in sleep.

The only word I can distinctly remember trying to teach Paul was the name "Jesus." I still recall my mother standing on the porch of our home telling me that she had gone to see the local parish priest to ask if Paul, who was then only three years old, could receive what in Catholic circles is called First Holy Communion. When my mother told me that the priest had promised that if Paul could simply say the name "Jesus" he would give him the bread of life, my task was sealed. Over and over, as I walked the sacred circle with Paul in my arms or rubbed his back gently as he lay in the crib, I spoke the name that is for Christians above all other names.

I loved Paul in the best way I knew how, at the time, by being present to help satisfy his needs. Who could have guessed that an innocent child would be the source of my greatest pain and necessary awakening—that I would come to discover in his face the face of Grace.

John Powers

As I leaned over Paul's crib night after night watching sleep hold him in the palm of its hand, how could I have known that through his living, laughing, and dying a host of passions would be aroused in me? It was love that gave my life meaning and loss that would give it depth.

LAND OF PAIN

For four years I tread, swam and drifted in the waters of Love and Loss until a rainy Saint Patrick's Day Sunday morning when Paul's death would slap me onto the Shore of Suffering in a rock-infested country called the Land of Pain.

The memories of that March morning are etched so deeply into the crevices of my being that I can still see my father carrying Paul into the bathroom to prepare him for a journey no one wanted him to take. Within half an hour my father was again gently carrying Paul's barely conscious body around the house, this time so that each family member could say what would be our last good-bye.

Sitting on the edge of my parents' bed I looked up to see Paul's head resting on my Father's strong shoulder and heard my father say, "Your mother and I are taking Paul to the hospital. He won't be coming home again."

Death slammed me against the sharp rocks in the harbor of the City of Chaos where I would wander bruised and broken. Paul's funeral service cut so deep into my heart that to survive I had to deny my feelings of anger, sadness, and fear. The only sound I heard or pain I felt during the Catholic services that promised my brother eternal life for his innocence was the closing of my heart.

Of course, I did not know at the time that the doors I closed within and behind me could not be locked. However, Grace knew, and from that moment began plotting for the day when she and life would not only help me open the closed doors in my heart but would also help me embrace the pain.

On the day Paul died it is estimated by the population division of the United Nations that worldwide 135,000 people died. My grief, however, was reserved exclusively for Paul since his was the only life that gave my life purpose and meaning.

Walking one day on Confusion Road in the City of Chaos I came upon, much to my surprise, a man I recognized, a fellow traveler in the Land of Pain.

Aquinas was a member of a local community

of Monks, properly known as the Passionists, but often more playfully called the Passionate Monks. Oddly, Aquinas happened to have visited my brother Paul in the hospital, chose to introduce himself to my parents, visited our home, and even offered me a job working as a waiter in the guest dining room at the Passionate Monastery.

"Excuse me, Aquinas," I said as I put out my hand, "but this is an amazing coincidence meeting you on this road just when I feel most lost."

"No it isn't," Aquinas responded. "Haven't you heard the story about a man lost at sea for many months and then stranded on a deserted island?"

"No I haven't," I answered.

"Well," he continued, "the man was deeply in love with a woman from his homeland, so much in love that when he found an empty bottle on the shore of the imprisoning island he took a rock and scratched out a message on a piece of bark, put the letter into the bottle and threw it into the ocean. The bottle drifted for many months until it finally washed ashore at the very feet of the woman he loved. When the woman saw the bottle she picked it up, opened it and read the message."

"What did it say?" I blurted out like a child.

"The message read, 'Dear Grace, There is no such a thing as a coincidence.' You see, John," Aquinas continued, "Grace is anti-chance, connecting us heart to heart, meaning to meaning. When I listened to my heart I heard, paradoxically, the beating of your pain. It was our friend Grace who told me that I could find you wandering on Confusion Road."

"You know Grace?" I asked.

"Of course I do. Any monk not in love with Grace is not a monk at all."

"Well, since you seem so familiar with this Land of Pain," I asked, "could you give me directions so that I can make my way back to my home on the Island of Ignorance? This Land is much too sharp and blunt. I'd be grateful if you could help me escape its borders."

"Ignorance Island is not your home," Aquinas answered. "Home is where the deepest part of your heart longs to belong, not where fear and insecurity drive you for temporary comfort. If you can't learn to live at home with yourself in the Land of Painful Reality then you'll never be at home with yourself anywhere.

"I'm sorry," he continued, "but I actually can't remember how to get to Ignorance Island anyway. I know I once lived there myself, but it's been many years since Grace awakened me to inner and outer reality. I honestly forget how to get there from here. If you'd like to travel with me, however, back to my home Monastery, perhaps we can find someone there who still remembers the way to the Island."

"Are there Monasteries on Ignorance Island, as well?" I asked.

"Oh yes," Aquinas answered. "There are a few Monasteries still left on the Island. I'm told, however, that there the Monks and people worship the little god of denial who they pray will take away the pain, uncertainty, and strug-gle of life.

"The problem, of course, is that although God is powerful enough to take away life's pain, to do so, God would have to take away the atmosphere of freedom. If God is, as many believe, the freedom that sets all others free, you can be sure God won't be helping anyone avoid responsibility or reality any time soon.

"If you really wish to escape the Land of Pain, I suggest," Aquinas continued, "you make your way to the Land of Fantasy. In the Churches, Synagogues, and Monasteries in Fantasy Land they practice a toxic faith that attempts to replace the natural world of feelings, bodiliness, and relationships with a supernatural world of perfection, purity, power, and orthodoxy.

"Of course, when your faith is healthy you naturally experience God in and through the works and wonders of the inner and outer worlds. When, however, you practice a toxic faith you must destroy the natural in order to feel significant or superior. Fantasy Land is, after all, the birthplace of racism, sexism, fundamentalism and all the other 'isms' that disgrace the God of the Universe.

"Since Ignorance Island, however, is actually only a broken off piece of Fantasy Land, perhaps we'll find someone along the way who has given up on reality and is returning there. It will be a difficult road to return to the Ignorance you once knew, however. In fact you may make the effort only to discover that you are no longer at home on the Island of Ignorance. Once the reality of love has formed you and death informed you, it is dangerous to heart and soul to try and live in Ignorance again.

"Ignorance can kill your soul, John," Aquinas continued, "cutting you off from the affirming presence of Grace forever. Suffering in the Land of Pain may seem unendurable to you now but with time and choice you can learn life's craftiest of arts, how to make your soul out of what you suffer. If you honestly wish to return to the

Lands of Fantasy or Ignorance I won't stop you. However, you're more than welcome, if you choose, to visit with the community of Monks with whom I live."

"I may go with you, Aquinas," I said, "to your Passionate Monastery, if you'll first tell me why you worship a God who reaches into life with the hand of death and takes innocent children out of the arms of those who love them. Explain to me why God has taken my brother, Paul, causing me and my family so much suffering. Defend your cruel God, Monk," I said with sarcasm, "and then I'll decide whether I'll visit your Monastery."

At first Aquinas ignored my hostile question, choosing instead to continue walking slowly and silently through the City of Chaos and out onto Catharsis Road.

When Aquinas finally did speak he did so in a lingering whisper that echoed from the beginning.

"We live in an age, John, when people expect God to explain and defend the existence of pain, suffering, and free will, yet these very same people feel no need to justify their own cruel words and violent acts.

"God did not take your brother," the Monk softly said. "I would not believe in such a callous God. The God I believe in, and have met through Grace, is not the God of death but the Lord of creativity. I believe in the God of life who shares, through Grace, all that God is with all creation.

"I'll tell you a secret about God that too few human beings dare to believe. The secret is that God is Aliveness and can't help but give aliveness to all creation, all the time, in fair measure. In fact, God gives more aliveness than human beings can take, and then, of course, asks of them more aliveness than they can give."

"Now wait a minute, Aquinas," I demanded. "If God is and gives only aliveness what is death?"

"Creative reorganization," Aquinas answered.

"Pass that by me again?" I asked.

"There really is no such thing as death," Aquinas replied, "if by death you mean the end of someone. You see, John, what you call death the universe calls creativity. Of course, you can judge death to be a violent form of creativity, a savage grace, but then God and the universe never promised to make decisions based on how it made human beings feel.

"What you perceive and judge as loss and destruction, John, God and the universe call the ongoing process of creative reorganizations of atoms, consciousness, and spirit.

"Certainly, John, your brother Paul's life has been dramatically and radically changed, but then," Aquinas continued, "the only thing constant about life is that it constantly changes. It seems Eve was right when she turned to Adam as they departed the Garden of Paradise and said, 'It looks like we live in an age of transition.'

"Of course, as you move along the eternal spiral of change, some transitions are more traumatic than others. Paul's aliveness, however, has not ended. In a sense you could say that your brother's life has been translated into a clearer language which you cannot as yet read or comprehend.

"I understand, John," Aquinas concluded, "how very much you want things to be as they were. That way Paul's physical presence would continue to secure your purpose and validate your existence.

"With Paul's death, however, life has changed for you, yet you refuse to change. It is because you refuse to live in the moment of now that you suffer. Most misery, after all, is caused by denying the reality of change."

"I admit," I responded hesitantly, "that I was happiest in life when I was taking care of Paul: talking, crying and even laughing with him. Paul made me feel needed and alive."

"I know, John," Aquinas said with a smile. "Paul has influenced your life in ways you are only now beginning to recognize. In fact we would not now be traveling together through the Land of Pain to the Passionate Monastery if it were not for Paul. Paul's life and death has shaped and shaken you into change. For this Grace you must be thankful. The paradox is, however, that the more you let go of your attachment to what Paul was for you, the more the memory of Paul will become a source of creativity."

"I can't imagine," I said pointedly, "ever being thankful that Paul has died."

"I did not say," Aquinas snapped back, "that you would be thankful for your brother's death. What I said was that you must be thankful for the impact Paul's life and death has and is having on your life, for the brutal gift of God's creative Grace.

"It is your love for Paul, after all, that will teach you to let go of him so that you can both continue to make life. It will take time for you to grieve your way to creativity, however. Accepting the fact that you must now wander and wonder in the Land of Pain, never to return to the Isle of Ignorance again, is enough for now."

IMAGI NATION

Is your Passionate Monastery much further?" I asked in an attempt to change the subject.

"No," Aquinas answered. "All we have to do is travel Catharsis Road until we come to the Mountain of Choice in the Land of Imagi Nation. My Monastery of Passion rests on a ledge only halfway up the mountain.

"Understand, however, that the Imagi Nation is not Fantasy Land. The Imagi Nation is the place where ideas, emotions, sensations, and spirit meet and mingle conspiring to create a nation of images to live there. To visit the Imagi Nation demands choice. You don't, however, choose to visit the Land of Fantasy. It overtakes you. Actually the Imagi Nation is only a short trip from anywhere."

"How will we know," I asked, "when we've crossed from the Land of Pain into the Imagi

Nation?"

"Oh," Aquinas answered, "that's easy. You can tell you're in the Imagi Nation by the colorful language that is spoken."

"I know," I said, "that in the Land of Pain the language of Hurt is spoken but what language do they speak in Imagi Nation?"

"Why, the mother tongue of Metaphor," Aquinas answered with a smile.

"Would it be possible," I asked, "for me to stay with you at the Monastery of Passion in Imagi Nation, at least until I've learned how religion can take away life's pain?"

"You can stay as long as you like in our Monastery," Aquinas answered. "You can even become a Monk if you choose. There is, however, no religion worthy of faith, that can take away the pain of life. Religion for security and safety sake is mere idolatry.

"Religion, John," Aquinas continued, "is useless without a spirituality that helps you live positively with pain and suffering. Healthy spirituality begins with this insight: We humans are incomplete, unfinished and imperfect. Recognizing your own confusion and imperfection is the first step on the journey home to yourself.

"Because what we share most is our human

weakness and frailty, suffering is something we must undergo, endure, and with the help of saving Grace thrive through.

"We suffer because we attempt to deny our unfinishedness, strive to avoid all pain, and fight to subdue God and the creative universe. The primary task of spirituality is to teach us to make home and soul out of the necessary freedom and inevitable pains that life offers.

"There are many people today, however," Aquinas pointedly said, "who misunderstand the relationship between religion and spirituality. The way I like to describe the interrelationship is that together they form a river. Religion is the solid banks and boundaries, the container of spiritual content, while spirituality is the fluid waters of divine perspective that flows always in the direction of life.

"Of course, from the confining banks perspective the water may seem at times to be uncontrollable and sloppy while from the waters perspective the boundaries may seem to be either a prison or a home. Only together, however, can they form a river.

"As religion and spirituality are distinct but not separate so too are the river's banks and water. A river without water is only a dry bed while water without banks floods away. In due season, spirituality, the divine perspective, flows into the banks of religion, flooding, drying up, and falling again.

"What you need most, John, what most people need most is the life-flowing spiritual vision that helps you move with reality rather than against it.

"You," Aquinas continued, "may, of course, enter the Monastery holding tight to the fantasy that you will find a God who will, if you worship correctly, take away the pain of living a human life only then to discover that in the very place you wish to hide, honesty lays waiting. The only God worth your worship is the God that helps you face your pain head-on, take it by the neck, and shake freedom and creativity from it.

"There are already far too many people who use religion to avoid life, who are addicted to a God of their wishes, a God who lifts them out of the world of feelings and flesh.

"Remember, John, that if you arrogantly cling to the illusion that by practicing a particular religion or even by joining a monastery you can escape the pain of love and loss, closet away your emotions, or ignore your body you will be sorely mistaken when life knocks you off your high horse. Of course, the struggle then will be to find a graceful way of standing up again. The Passionate community has helped me find my way.

"You see, John," Aquinas continued, "healthy Passionate spirituality does not despise negative or positive emotions, motivating passions, or the body, as so many of the so-called religiously inclined do today, nor does it compartmentalize a relationship with God into a private affair, but rather the community to which I belong teaches us to direct the flow of feelings and passions into making the world a just, free, and safe home for all to live in."

"But isn't God's job to make me feel better?" I asked.

"No," Aquinas answered. "The God I believe in will help you live with and through how you feel but will not take your feelings away. The God I believe in will give you the creative energy to live with and learn from the small and large transitions of life.

"Of course, while Grace's primary responsibility is to teach, yours, John, is to learn. Therefore, as a real citizen of the Imagi Nation you can find Grace mentoring where God wills, in shopping malls and monasteries, to monks and moms equally.

"However, if you choose to live in our

Passionate Monastery, John," Aquinas concluded, "I guarantee that Grace will teach you,
through your sisters and brothers in the Passion,
the finest of living arts, how to convert the passion of suffering and agony into a passion for
creative life and soul-making."

I traveled with Aquinas on Catharsis Road
until we came to the Monastery of Passion, in
Imagi Nation. The choice to climb the mountain on which the Monastery was perched was
not an easy one, however. The desire for ignorance and fantasy had not yet left me, but
seemed only to have temporarily eased in the
presence of my wise and courageous mentor.

If it were possible, however, to live creatively
instead of steeped in grief, I was willing to try.
When I mentioned to Aquinas that I might
answer the call to become a Monk, joining the
Kinship of the Passion he answered with a question.

"Why?"

"Well," I said, "because I believe God is calling me, that it is my destiny to belong to the
Brethren of the Passion."

"Any other reason?" Aquinas asked.

"Not that I'm aware of," I said.

"Perhaps, as we discussed earlier," Aquinas
answered, "you merely wish to hide from the

pain of life in a fortress of security, or want to please your parents, gain respect from society, are afraid to love again after losing, or perhaps you're motivated by a combination of all the above. I haven't met a human being yet who is not marvelously mixed in motives. If you honestly hope to become a Monk, however, you must become aware of all that drives you.

"Actually, John," Aquinas continued, "I'm not sure God calls anyone to become a Monk. I know God calls everyone to become loving human beings, to use their gifts where there is need, but how each one chooses to follow this universal vocation is up to the freedom and preference of each person. While the call to love is persistently universal the response can only be individual.

"In my experience, there are only two valid reasons for becoming a Monk, or for that matter a lawyer, parent, plumber, friend or professor. The first is because, whatever your choice, it is the only way you feel you can adequately, or even inadequately, express your love and use your gifts. The second reason is because it's fun. It's fun to be a monk," Aquinas said with a sly smile. "It's the way I love life and hopefully add love to life.

"If you can say the same, John, then feel free

to join the Brethren of the Passion. Remember, however, the freer you are to choose, the more authentic the life. If you aren't free enough to say 'no' to becoming a Monk, your 'yes' will mean little or nothing at all.

"Live the life that is yours, John," Aquinas continued, "not the life others wish for you. And try to listen to God's heart beating in your heart, for in the trying will be the dying to all the motives that are not true to you as well as the rising of who you already are. Let Grace be with you on this trying journey."

After climbing our way up the Mountain of Choice, passing such other tempting side roads as Addiction Avenue, Compulsion Circle, Fear Boulevard, and Laziness Street, Aquinas and I arrived at the Passionate Monastery. Standing outside the large glass doors that let you easily see inside, we stopped to read a message chiseled into a stone above the entrance.

Once Aquinas told me that he never entered the Monastery without reading the message aloud, I joined him in the proclamation. "Without Passion there is no Life."

I entered the Monastery of the Passion and have remained there till this day, learning in the remembering, studying what has been written about God and life, listening to the stories others have to tell describing how through faith it is possible to enjoy aliveness on the journey through the Land of Pain and wondering whether I will ever belong to myself enough to feel at home wherever I am.

With my curiosity piqued by the Monk's talk of converting the passion of pain into a passion for possibility I decided to learn everything I could about this mysterious art. It seemed impossibly magical that anyone could learn to travel in the Land of Pain without suffering so I decided to study what I thought was a secret of the saints.

Not only did I read every book I could find in the Monastery library on the subjects of soul, psyche, and about what one Monk called "God's psychotherapy"—prayer—I also studied the story of how Jesus loved His way through the Land of Crucifying pain and death into the sacred Imagi Nation where aliveness and creativity were resurrected again.

For the Monks and I, Jesus was the exemplar of one who rose through suffering to new life. Not only was I inspired by the story of how Jesus faced the suffering Passion of His own life, and by drawing strength from the pain transformed the energy of misery into an even stronger and more passionate urge to make life for those who suffer, but I learned that I was required by destiny to do the same.

When finally, after years of preparation, I vowed myself to the Passionate Community I promised not only to do what Jesus did, converting the passion of pain into a passion for life but I promised also to tell the tale of the Crucified One of yesterday and the crucifieds of today.

Because Aquinas believed that the best way to tell the story of the Crucifieds is by telling the story of your own inner life of dying and rising he came to me with an odd suggestion.

Since I seemed so intent on learning the art of conversion, of exchanging the passion of pain for the passion of possibility, he recommended that I meet with a talented psychotherapist on the Bridge of Therapy just outside the gates of the Monastery.

"The therapist," Aquinas said, "will help you find within yourself what you cannot find in books, your own story of pain and potential."

When I, at first, resisted the idea that I needed a psychotherapist to help me become a Monk, Aquinas simply said:

"The more important task is to become a gracious human being, a free man. In order to become a man, however, you must face the greatest challenge, tell the tale of your secret pain. If you walk the bridge where secrets are remembered and told you may just discover hidden in the package of your grief the gift of creativity, the very capacity to make life.

"In the exchange of stories, John, you may be changed," Aquinas concluded, "for in the telling is the transformation. Off with you, now, to the Bridge of Therapy on Catharsis Road. The storylistener, the Artist of Psyche, expects to see you at the appointed time."

BRIDGE OF THERAPY

Although I was quite fearful of the unknowns of the psychotherapeutic process I trusted the wise mentor Aquinas enough to take his advice and meet with the Artist of Psyche on the Bridge of Therapy just below and around the bend from the Passion Monastery.

I knew precisely where the bridge was located on the Mountain of Choice since Aquinas had pointed it out to me many times over the years as we traveled up and down the rough mountain. In fact, if I looked out my windows on the top floor of the Monastery I could easily see the towers that marked the middle of the bridge and where I presumed the Artist practiced his healing craft.

While climbing down the mountain to, as the Brethren called it, "Transition Bridge," I wondered if the Artist would try to convince me that there was no God. I'd heard that many

Psych-Artists believed that God was at least a silly illusion if not a self-destructive delusion. I put this worrisome thought out of my mind, however, when I recalled something Aquinas had said: "that the wish for God may just, after all, be hooked onto a reality and that you should never deny in the Land of Pain what you've seen in the Imagi Nation."

As I walked halfway across Transition Bridge to the Tower of Therapy for my first appointment with the Artist I'd never have guessed that I was beginning what would become a rugged two-and-a-half year journey, meeting twice a week, with a clever and compassionate master of the psyche as my guide.

While waiting for a response to my knock on the narrow wooden door of the bridge tower I noticed a posted sign hanging on the wall off to the left. Taking a step back to focus on the message I read,

> WELCOME. IF YOU'RE EARLY YOU'RE ANXIOUS, IF YOU'RE ON TIME YOU'RE COMPULSIVE, IF YOU'RE LATE YOU'RE RESISTING. YOU CAN'T WIN. WINNING, HOWEVER, IS NOT THE POINT. THE POINT IS TO STOP HIDING FROM AND LYING TO YOURSELF.

"Welcome," a tall white haired gentleman said, after the tower door swung open. "Please come in," he said, as we shook hands and looked into each other's eyes. "Follow me," he continued as he led me through the tower. "This is the Room of Remembrance," he said as we came to a halt in a glass-enclosed porch. "Please have a seat," he said, as he pointed my way to a large red leather chair about six feet from his own.

As I settled comfortably in my chair I felt as though I'd met the Artist of Psyche before. It was something about the tone of his voice or the graceful manner of his movements.

"Tell me about yourself, John," the Artist said, interrupting my déjà vu.

One question was all I needed to begin telling story after story about my mother and father, brothers and sisters to prove that I was the normal one in my family, perhaps even gifted, at least, the special one.

To my whining and moaning, complaining and entertaining stories about my family the Artist commonly raised an eyebrow, smiled slightly, nodded his head, or hummed a note to keep me telling my tale.

Trained to listen to not only what I was saying but also to what I was not the Artist practiced his craft well, speaking up only to prod my remembering.

After many months of weaving stories about my growing-up years in a family of nine, the Artist gently asked again.

"So, tell me about yourself."

Although I felt a bit uncomfortable with his repetitious question I again responded without hesitation. This time, however, with many more months of new stories—comedies, romances, dramas and tragedies—all to capture what it was like to live in the Church family, to study in a Seminary, to live with fifty-odd men in a large stone Monastery, and to compete with some of the most saintly and most sinful for God's and the Church's attention and approval.

As I rambled on about the Monks I liked or disliked as well as about those who liked or disliked me the Artist of Psyche wrapped his attention around me. No one had ever listened so intently to me before. Surprisingly it was the act of his listening that seduced me into a deeper self-revelation.

"So, John, tell me about yourself," the Artist asked for the third time.

"What do you think I've been doing twice a week for the last year?" I said with more anger than I'd realized was waiting there.

"Tell me about the members of your inner family," the Artist said. "About the kin within you, the 'homunculi,' the constellating characters and little people that rent space in your inner world."

"What are you talking about?" I asked, hoping that he'd respond with a simple nod or twitch of the eyebrow. Instead the Artist sat forward and after his chair stopped creaking said,

> 'Within my earthly temple there's a
>   crowd;
> There's one of us that's humble, one
>   that's proud,
> There's one that's broken-hearted for
>   his sins,
> There's one that's unrepentant, sits
>   and grins;
> There's one that loves his neighbor as
>   himself
> And one that cares for naught but
>   fame and wealth.
> From much corroding care I should
>   be free
> If I could once determine which is
>   me?'[2]

"So, John, tell me how you feel?" he asked.

Tears baptized me into the community of the honest as my most painful and secret feelings sprang free from the closet of fear.

Some ten years after the death of my brother Paul Joseph I finally allowed myself to feel the pain, to not only grieve his death but to grieve the loss of life as I'd wished it would be.

In session after session I relived the moments of Paul's life and death. I recalled through tears of laughter how I tried to entertain Paul with play to distract him from his pain and through sobs of sorrow how gently I held him when it all seemed too much. I told of watching my father at Paul's wake service bend a knee to the floor during a recited Hail Mary prayer, followed then by his tears and head falling into his hands. I confessed that, at the time, the best, or better put, the worst I could do was sob silently, shedding dry-eyed tears between decades of the Rosary.

"I miss Paul," I said, as I grieved through many more months of therapy, sharing one feeling, one member of my inner household after another. "I feel guilt that he died while I lived, rage at God and life for taking him from me and my family, regret that I couldn't do more to save him, and shame for not being able to hide my feelings like a man is taught to do."

Finally, after almost two years of sessions in the Room of Remembrance I said, "I set you free, Paul, free to live as you are. After all, all there is is aliveness, isn't there?" I asked. "As long as God lives doesn't everything live? I promise to remember you, Paul, for you have the right to be remembered, the right to be remembered as you truly were and not merely as I wished you had been, the right to be prayed to and for through the aliveness of God, and finally the right to be judged by God alone."

I may not have realized it at the time but by setting Paul Joseph free I set myself free, not from my brother but from the tyranny of my grief.

As I embraced my pain and loss the Artist of Psyche embraced me, setting both Paul and me free to live with the life that was ours.

Suddenly, while wrapped in the Artist's strength I remembered who he reminded me of. "Of course," I thought. It was the soft sound of his voice that reminded me of the Grace of God. No sooner had I imagined her but there she was, fully present.

"Let me share a few secrets with you, John," Grace said. "In fact, since you've been talking so much in therapy, why don't you just listen for a while. The first secret happens to be about secrets.

"You see, John," Grace continued, "keeping secrets isn't good or bad, healthy or sick. It's just something human beings use to survive in a society that is all about judging and measuring human worth and value.

"The best kept secret of all, though, is that every human being keeps the same secret, a fear of loneliness and rejection if they ever reveal their secrets. Humans beings share the same murderous and joyful thoughts, loving or lustful passions and are, therefore, not unique. The deepest kept secret of all is that human beings are all kept and controlled by the same feelings.

"What you tend to hide is, of course," Grace continued, "the very stuff society or family tells you should never be shared, the shameful and glorious failures and successes, weaknesses and strengths, evil intents and spiritual insights. Not only are you taught to hide the so-called wicked thoughts but you're also taught to repress the more sublime, love, self-esteem and, of course, me.

"Actually, most people don't so much keep secrets as much as they are kept by them. Afraid of being rejected or shunned if the truth be known, secret-keepers are already trapped by what they run from, fear.

"If the truth be told, however, life flourishes only in the truth. Sadly, it seems human beings only learn to tell the truth to themselves, and appropriately to others, when the pain of keeping secrets becomes greater than the pain or consequences of disclosure."

"Pain," I said interrupting. "That's precisely why I decided to go along with Aquinas' suggestion that I meet with the Artist of Psyche. You see, Grace," I continued, "I thought therapy might help me find my way out of the Land of Pain."

"I'm surprised you stayed quiet for as long as you did, John," Grace answered, "but living creatively in the Land of Pain happens to be the subject of the second secret I wanted to tell you.

"While you, John, along with just about everyone else in the world spend your time trying to get out of the Land of Pain, pain is trying to teach you something. You see, John," Grace continued, "pain plays an important function in your life. The secret is that pain is a guide, not an enemy.

"Pain warns you of physical danger, telling you that there is something wrong. In fact, psychic pain is nature's way of telling you that you're out of balance. Every pain tells you something about yourself. The task of therapy," Grace continued, "is not to help you escape the Land of your Pain but to help you learn from it so that you can live more creatively with yourself and others.

"After all is said and done, the greatest cause of suffering is not pain, but the desire to avoid all pain. Face your secret desire to escape and you set your creative passions free to help you make life where you are, instead of always seeking an Island of comfortable Ignorance.

"As far as I'm concerned, John," Grace continued, "the most creative people in the world are not necessarily those who write books, paint, birth, or even parent a child, but rather they're those who name and befriend the demons and angels that live in their own psyches.

"You can never be free to live creatively," Grace continued, "whether in the Land of Pain or in the Imagi Nation until you let the feelings, thoughts, and desires that manipulate, motivate, and control you tell their stories.

"That's why," Grace concluded, "you've been visiting the Artist of Psyche for these past few years, John, to hear your own secrets and story."

"Is that," I asked, "the third secret you wanted to tell me, Grace, that therapy is about listening to your selves?"

"Partially," Grace responded. "My last secret, however, has more to do with the great lie, the most vicious and cunning deception that human beings can inflict upon themselves and each other. The lie proclaims that you are how you feel, what you think, want, desire, or need at the moment. The secret, however, is that you can never be true to yourself if all you do is follow your every feeling.

"You see, John," Grace continued, "you have feelings but you are more than your feelings. When you fall prey to the deception that you are how you feel, you suffer. Every minuscule morsel of misery in life is caused by the perverse notion that you are how you feel.

"Identity is, after all, more than feelings and thoughts, more than wants and wishes. Identity is something far more permanent than the 126 bits of information that pass through your central nervous system every second.[3]

"Of course, it is essential for choice and life to listen to your passions and feelings, to get to know your inner household well, but to follow them? Only if they make life.

"After all, who you are," Grace said, "is distinct from your emotions, passions, thoughts, sensations, and body but, then again, not separate from them either.

"Identity, however, has to do with the source of all information, consciousness, and creativity that lives between the pieces and bits that flow through awareness, the deeper power, the eternal motivator, God."

"So, tell me about yourself?" the Artist of Psyche asked again, this time interrupting Grace's lecture.

"In one moment of revealed imaginings," I replied, "I not only saw myself sitting before the members of my own psyche; the grief that haunted me, the fear that drove me, the desire that seduced me, the arrogance that closeted me, and the persistent urge to ignore and escape reality, but I experienced the Immanent Reality of God, living deepest within and beyond my psyche.

"I knew," I continued, "that in that numenous moment I was present to an 'Other,' beyond yet revealed in the Imagi Nation. I knew then," I said, "that God is not any of the little *me's* that frequently fight for control of my inner household but is rather a reality as much within me as without me."

Having finished my reply I fell silent, joining the Artist's quiet presence. Then after looking deep into each other's eyes for what seemed like an hour the Artist said:

"In George Bernard Shaw's play, *St. Joan*, Joan says in response to a French officer's question: 'I hear voices tell me what to do.' The captain replies, 'They come from your imagination.' St. Joan again answers, saying 'Of course. That is how the messages of God come to us'"[4]

"As an Artist of Psyche, John, I could never use the words 'just' or 'merely' to describe the Imagi Nation. I learned many years ago to respect the power of imagining as almost sacred, perhaps as divinity itself.

"Having said that, I must also tell you," he continued, "that although as a therapist I might be able to help you heal inner conflicts, build a healthier kinship within your psyche, which will, of course, help you build a stronger kinship with others, as far as a kinship with God? That you will have to seek in God's psychotherapy. While I may help you find freedom from the selves that oppress you, leading you perhaps to the door of God, you must open that door yourself. You must discern and distinguish for yourself the different voices you hear speaking in and through your Imagi Nation."

After two and a half years of psyche work, crossing back and forth between pain and possibility on the Bridge of Therapy, I said good-bye to the Artist of Psyche for the last time.

Although I terminated our therapeutic relationship I continue to be influenced by his remembered presence. Our relationship has certainly changed but it has not ended. I can still hear the Artist's voice echoing in the Land of Imagi Nation.

I will never describe my years of psychotherapy in the Room of Remembrance as easy. In fact, it was the most difficult work I've ever done. It has also been, however, the most rewarding. Why? You might wonder. Well, because it's possible to find freedom and the God that creates all reality free while telling and listening to your own story.

Of course, I still miss my brother Paul Joseph, especially his unlived life. I'm also, at times, still ambushed by my grief. There is, however, a difference now. Because I'm a bit more aware of the sadness and loneliness that lurk within my inner household I can let these feelings pass; I can be free to live with the missing.

This, of course, does not mean that I am fully aware of all my feelings, needs and drives, however. In fact, the desire to return to the Island of Ignorance or at least to visit the Land of Fantasy for a bit of pleasure, power, prestige, position, or pennies still moves me.

SUCCESS CITY

After nine years of living with the Brethren of the Passion on the Mountain of Choice studying philosophy, theology and psychology including the two and a half years crossing Therapy Bridge I found myself standing on a hillside, overlooking the City of Success, a megatropolis that sits firmly on the borders of the Imagi Nation and the Land of Fantasy.

Proceeding into the gleaming city, successfully professed a Passionate Monk and ordained a Catholic Priest I took up the tasks of preaching the Word, presiding at public God encounters while helping people search passionately for the God of life.

Although I already had arrived at the goal of my dreams by becoming a Monk and Priest I was not satisfied. There was one more dream to be lived, one that moved me confidently down Ambition Street into the inner City of Success.

I wanted to become an Artist of the Psyche, a psychotherapist.

Fueled by mixed motives, as is every traveler on Ambition Street—the mix at times made of seventy percent an altruistic desire to serve and thirty percent a low self-esteem need to prove myself, while at other times thirty percent altruism and seventy percent arrogance—I sped through the City going nowhere fast.

In fact, now that I think about it, I've never met a traveler on any of life's many roads toward Success City who's fueled by only a single motive. There's always more than one inner voice urging us on toward our goals.

There is, of course, nothing wrong with dreaming, with wanting to achieve, with the desire to live in Success City. In fact, in the Imagi Nation everyone has the right to choose the dreams they follow, to decide where they want to live.

When you travel in Fantasy Land, however, you have no choice. Your dreams, fueled by need, become nightmares, driving you along Ambition Street until you either satisfy your desire or run out of need, neither of which ever happens.

Fueled by the dream and the need to become an Artist of the Psyche I immediately after becoming a Monk and Priest asked and begged the Administrator Monks of Funds and Personnel for the Passionate Community to grant me permission, leave from work, and the money to pursue studies toward my new goal.

Because, however, I'd already studied for nine years to become a Priest member of the Community of Monks, the Passionate Administrators decided that before I could add another three to five years to my schooling history I should work as a Priest and Preacher for a few years.

For a variety of what, I believe, were at times justifiable and at other times rather vague reasons, each of my requests for studies were denied until the seventh year when not only was my petition granted but I was encouraged to apply to any psycho-studies program in the world I choose.

Unaware that I'd already hitched my identity, my "I am," to my feelings of inferiority and self-doubt I found myself driven up Ambition Street in the Fantasy Land of Success City by my need for position, prestige, and power. No longer was I making free choices. Instead, choices were made for me by my desire to achieve, by my unconscious urge to make who I am out of what I do.

Of course, I would apply only to the program of studies that everyone traveling Ambition Road agreed was the most prestigious in Church circles, the University of Rome in Success City.

After nine years of priestly work, the last five of which were spent in the very stressful ministry of Radio and Television Preaching, working twelve to fourteen hour days, six or seven days a week, producing, writing, hosting, and trying to fund three religious radio and television programs, editing a monthly magazine and writing books, while regularly ignoring time for prayer, rest and health all to prove that I was worth spending the time and money on for further training, I finally turned the last corner on Ambition Street into the inner City of Success arriving in Rome to take up studies at Success U.

I'd become a workaholic, dependent upon the work I did for identity and value, while paradoxically on my way to learn how to set others free from their dependencies.

The paradox was so thick I got stuck in the conflict of mixed motives. Since, however, you can only take others as far as you've traveled yourself, it was impossible for me to set anyone else free without first finding emotional and spiritual liberty.

For almost nine weeks, in the most brutally humid July and August air I'd ever breathed I roamed the Roman streets, practiced the Italian language in preparation for my living and studying, and did my priestly work saying over and over again, "no problem," to every new cultural and academic challenge.

While standing on the corner of Satisfaction and Ambition Streets in the City of Success I couldn't help but think that I'd finally arrived. I'd reached my goal, I thought, fulfilled my dream, accomplished the plan, got what I wanted. Or did I?

Suddenly, without warning—or could it be that what was about to happen was the warning—I couldn't remember what I was doing or where I was going in the City. I literally, at one point, sat on the landing of the Spanish steps in the Piazza di Spagna in the heart of the Roman City of Success—going up or down I did not know which—unable to remember my name or how to get back home.

There I sat for hours not only trying to remember who and where I was but also desperately trying to determine what was happening to me. Was it a breakdown, I wondered, or a breakthrough? In the midst of all my confusion the only words I could clearly hear myself saying were, "I can't imagine myself working for the next five years as hard as I've worked the last seven. I can't imagine it. I can't imagine it." I repeated it over and over. Finally my mind agreed with my body and I said, "I can't go on this way."

Little did I know when I reached the inner City of Success that I would run headlong into the Wall of Limitations, that I would run out of the fuel of need and desire, that I would burn out of the mental, physical and spiritual energy needed to keep going, that the fast track would lead me where it leads all fools—into Failure Ditch just off Ambition Street in the Fantasy section of Success City.

Obviously, life and the Grace that fills it doesn't have to hit me over the head to get my attention. They have to hit me again and again and then one more time for good measure. Because while traveling Ambition Street I hadn't given my spirit, mind, and body the normally required rest, recreation, and time for renewal, they revolted, shutting down all but necessary activity in order to protect what energy was left. I was sick enough that my body and mind burned out to protect themselves from extinction.

Victimized and beaten by my own need to reach Success City at all cost I lay worn-out, exhausted and wounded in Failure Ditch, unable to move. The body never lies.

I cried out to a fellow Priest as he marathoned by, moving faster on Ambition Street than I thought possible, but he looked at me with fear in his eyes and sped on his way.

There were other Brethren of the Passion and friends, however, with whom I shared my story of failure who encouraged me to do what was best for body, psyche, and soul, to show the same compassion toward myself that I'd shown and preached about to others.

While lying in the dust of loneliness in Failure Ditch burned out of strength and confidence, perhaps I should have known from experience that I was not alone.

"So, we meet again," Aquinas said as he bent down to help me to my feet. "What brings you," he asked, "to Failure Ditch, my friend?"

"Well," I choked, trying to clear my throat of shame. "After years of traveling on Ambition Street I finally arrived in the City of Success only to find myself so sick of being driven by my need to prove myself worthy and tired of chasing after the dream that I fell exhausted into Failure Ditch."

"Everyone," Aquinas said as he shrugged his

shoulders, "needs a little downtime. Even someone as notable as Sisyphus knows that. Enjoy the opportunity, John."

"What's Sisyphus got to do with this?" I said as I shook the dust of loneliness from my cloths.

"You know who Sisyphus is?" Aquinas asked.

"Of course," I replied. "He's the Greek character who was punished with the eternal task of pushing a huge boulder up a hill after tricking the gods into making him immortal."

"Sisyphus," Aquinas said, "is still pushing his rock up the Hill of Achievement in the Imagi Nation. Of course, when he gets close to the top, where the hill is naturally the steepest, he loses control of the boulder and it rolls right back down the hill."

"I get it," I said. "You call the time it takes Sisyphus to walk down the hill after his rock 'downtime.' Cute."

"I thought so," Aquinas said. "In fact I'd say the point is sharp enough to deserve a laugh."

"No time for laughter now," I said. "Perhaps later. Right now I'd like you to guide me back to Success City, if you can."

"There's a real rush on Success City these days, that's for sure," Aquinas remarked to no one in particular as he turned toward the traffic on Ambition Street. "By the way," he said as he turned quickly back to look at me, "what was it you were chasing after anyway, John?"

"I wanted to become an Artist of the Psyche," I replied.

"Why?" he asked.

"I'm not sure anymore," I answered. "I think I wanted to set people free as I'd been set free in therapy but then again," I continued, "I also liked the position of authority the title Artist of Psyche could give.

"I wanted to build hope, but then again, I also wanted to make my life easier, to feel more important, to bury my feelings under a pile of accomplishments. I wanted to serve and be served." Finally, I said in response. "Now that you ask, Aquinas, I'm not sure anymore exactly why I wanted to become an Artist of Psyche."

"That's the problem then," Aquinas answered. "If you'd remembered to stay close to your original altruistic desire to share freedom with others you would not only have arrived in Success City but you would have taken up residence.

"After all, John," Aquinas continued, "Ambition Street isn't a self-destructive highway but one of many roads that leads to Success City. Whether you make the journey on Determination, Passion, Perseverance, or Ambition streets doesn't matter as much as whether you are fueled and motivated by the greed to get or the hope of giving."

"As usual," I said in response, "I'm terribly graced to have run into you again, Aquinas. With your keen sense of direction I'm sure you can point the way out of Failure Ditch and into the heart of Success City."

"Let's meander along Ambition Street together, John," Aquinas replied. "Perhaps we'll hear what the Grace of failure has to teach you along the way."

"You're not," I asked, "going to try and convince me that failure has its hidden blessings, are you?"

"Yes, I am," Aquinas said. "In fact, I've found that failure can actually save lives. It's not uncommon, John," he continued, "for illness, exhaustion, burnout or a crisis of confidence to provide people with the very exit they were looking for to get off the fast track of expectation.

"When I say, however, that you can find benefits even in the failure experience I'm not trying to pull a Pollyanna on you. I'm not implying either that you wouldn't turn back the clock if you could but rather that in the intensified climate of failure and crisis not only can growth accelerate but you too can learn, what millions of others have learned, that within the failure experience lies the mystery of success.

"Failure is, of course, something healthy people prefer to avoid," Aquinas said, "but when it's staring you right in the face I think it's best to listen and learn from it."

"If failure is such a graceful mentor, what," I asked, "has she taught you, Aquinas?"

"She's taught me," Aquinas immediately responded, "to take care of myself during the dark times that live between life's lights. Failure is at worst a time in between, at best a rest stop on Ambition Street. It does not have to be a destination.

"Failure," Aquinas lectured, "is a time to sort out priorities and reassess values, to ask questions rather than give answers, to leave as many doors open to the past and future as possible, to rest at work and work at resting, to pay attention to what you're doing so that you won't be so easily caught up in the glamour of overactivity but will rather work with a steady pressure on the wheel that will slowly get you where you truly want to go.

"The Grace of failure has taught me in the in-between time," he continued, "to remember how small my mind is, how big my limitations are, and how absolutely essential it is to turn in prayers and meditation toward a bigger mind than mine.

"Failure, after all, is not a permanent condition, a fatal flaw, a fall from Grace, contagious social disease or condemnation of character, but is rather a judgement of an event or happening in life.

"The experience of having failed, hitting bottom, blowing your chance, breaking down or going bust, in other words, every disruptive and dysfunctional stage you pass through in life—which is what failure is, a stage—can teach you to be more flexible and adaptive to the external circumstances of life, to reconsider the image you have of yourself, to examine whether the expectations of others have become your necessity, to affirm the relationships in your life by spending more time with those you love and, finally, to confirm your purpose in life by doing the work you love.

"Failure, John," Aquinas continued, "reminds you that you must reinvent your inner and outer self throughout life, to redefine who you are and what you are about. Through the process of falling down and getting up again you can learn how important it is for you to write your own life story rather than being written off by society's myths of success and failure.

"Ultimately," Aquinas concluded, "the crisis

and failures of life have taught me to have faith in myself, others, and the God of and beyond my understanding. Any experience in life that does that, even failure, is Grace-filled.

"You may have failed, John," Aquinas said, "but you are not a failure. There is a difference. You are only a failure if you identify who you are with this crisis experience, if you take this failure personally.

"Tell me, John," he asked, "do you regret your decision to leave the beautiful Roman City?"

"No," I said, with only a moment's hesitation. "My decision to leave the Success City of Rome after burning out was a decision for survival sake. I couldn't continue the pace my low self-esteem had set for me.

"As I've heard said," I continued, "there's only one thing worse than not getting what you want and that is getting what you want.

"I got what I wanted, permission to go on for studies. To do so, however, I worked myself into burnout. I guess failure requires some effort, after all.

"One thing I am sure of, though, is that if I'd stayed in the University program I would eventually have been either committed to a House of Therapy or done major damage to soul and body.

"The only decision I regret along the way, I said, "is that I didn't take care to listen to the many selves in my inner household, to my body and spirit long before I left for Rome. I regret not taking care of myself.

"Let's hope, however, that this Roman experience of failure will teach me as much about my own psyche as would an academic program of studies at Success U.

"At this point," I concluded, "I'm just thankful that I've survived another fall, that I endured the pain of failure."

"The more important question," Aquinas said, "is whether you will thrive through the failure. To crumble or stop functioning in a crisis is quite normal for a time. Ultimately, though, you must look deeply into yourself, listen to your true needs and feelings, and imagine yourself moving on. Survival spirituality is for those who believe in only themselves. Thriver spirituality is for those who walk with Grace. It is Grace, after all, who gives you the courage to wrestle your failure to the ground wrenching strength and freedom from its grip.

"Whatever you do in life, John," Aquinas continued, "whether you are a priest, psychotherapist, postal clerk, bottle washer, lawyer, or parent, if the creative work you do is to be a part of a spiritual search it must be passionately directed toward goals that are greater than the need to please others or the greed for happiness. What you do must come from who you are and what you love, not from a need to measure up to the believed expectations of others. If you follow what you love and do what is most loving, happiness happens. You cannot steal happiness from life, however, by playing competitive games of success and failure.

"The real failures of this world," Aquinas continued, "are those who measure success by how much pleasure, position, power, prestige, or pennies they can gather to themselves. The more you judge yourself by the standards of a society fixated on what you accomplish, and by how much money or power you acquire in the doing of what you do, the sicker you become. If you let society judge whether you are a success or failure, sick or healthy, you have already failed.

"After all, the normal fall apart when the burdens of life are too heavy while the abnormal arrogantly refuse to respect stress and realistic limitations. Only when you accept that the measure of failure and success are in you, will you live balanced enough so that no situation, external event, or person can disturb or control you.

"Remember, John," Aquinas continued, "no matter what change you make on the outside, you won't be successful until you face the inner tyrants of low self-esteem, self-pity, and fear that control and oppress you. The truly successful learn first to live well within themselves.

"If you must measure whether someone is successful in the human adventure look for their creativity to tolerate the pain of falling down and getting up and falling down and getting up again, whether they have the insight into themselves to learn from life's pain, whether they have an independence of spirit that gives them the freedom to depend on others when appropriate but the skill to set proper limits on the expectations others have of them, the ability to make and keep friends, and whether they respect themselves enough to believe in a God beyond themselves."

"With all my training as a Monk, a Priest, and a would-be Artist of the Psyche," I said, "you'd think I could have avoided being overwhelmed by the fantasy that if I merely pleased others or worked hard enough I could get what I wanted. Stupidly, I became a slave to my own desires for approval, acting as though I had it all together when in reality I'd forgotten where I put my frail humanity."

"You know, John," Aquinas said, "that it's not what you know that makes you a success but who you know, beginning, of course, with knowing yourself. It's knowledge of the heart and inner family that determines success or failure.

"You must understand, that just because someone becomes a Monk, worships every day or sabbath in church or synagogue, or says that they believe in God and dogma does not exempt them from the human condition.

"After all," Aquinas said, "the greatest miracle of all is that in the practice of faith, no matter where and when you turn your life over to God, God will always give it right back to you. That way you'll have something to wrestle with for the rest of your life."

"I can be a slow learner," I said, as Aquinas and I turned a corner on Ambition Street, finding ourselves, much to my surprise, standing before the front doors of the Monastery of Passion on the Mountain of Choice.

"What are we doing here?" I asked. "I thought you were leading me back to Success City."

"Success City, John," Aquinas replied, "is found in your own backyard. Actually, it's everywhere, if you have faith in yourself, others and God.

"Let's," he suggested, "read aloud the saying above the door."

After reading together, "Without Passion There is no Life," we entered the Passionate Monastery to walk the silence-stained corridors of tile and stone. As we climbed the staircase to the second floor Aquinas made the following sound recommendation.

"Your messing up, your failure, John, would not seem so terrible to you if you realized how little it really matters to others and to God. What matters most is what you do with the mess you make. Ultimately, failure is a wound that lets God in, a crack in the armor through which Grace can move. The best place to take failure, therefore, is to prayer, where God is always giving you what you need most, graceful courage."

I don't know why I was surprised to arrive at the door to the Chapel of Prayer in the Monastery of Passion after the many unexpected turns in my journeys with Aquinas, but I was.

"You may be even more surprised," Aquinas said before continuing down the corridor, "to find a lifelong friend waiting for you inside."

CHAPEL OF PRAYER

As I reached to open the heavy oak Chapel door my eyes drifted upward to read the calligraphic words etched into the stucco wall. As I read the familiar, but all too easily forgotten phrase, I felt the words almost grab me by the throat and shake me. They said, *God works with what God's got.*

As I entered and sat down in the back pew of the Chapel my memory began to replay old praying tapes when I thought that in prayer my expectation would become God's necessity. When hurt, for example, I would run to God to demand that God not only take away the pain but give me comfort as well. When I felt that the struggle of life was too frustrating I begged God to explain why. As a young man and monk I'd felt far more sure of who God was, primarily because I'd commanded God be who I needed God to be for me.

Since before the beginning, long before the Word, there was only silence, I closed my eyes and opened my heart to listen to what God had to say in the quiet of the Chapel.

After only a few minutes of inner rest I could almost hear the millions of prayer requests left to hang loosely in the spiritual atmosphere. The room was a marvel of woods stained with the shadows and prayers of the passing years. Just then, gently, oh so very gently, I heard the whispering voice of Grace say to me:

"Prayer doesn't get you more of the God you want but rather prayer is a relationship with the Perpetual Presence that is beyond imagining, emotion, thoughts, and desires, yet is revealed through these distinctively human capacities. A prayerful relationship with the Presence gives you the capacity to distinguish between the gods of your own making and the God that is encouraging you to make your life out of the chaos you've got and the mess you've made.

"Healthy religion is forever about letting go of the images of what God should be so that you can be free to relate to the God that is. To tell you the truth, I'm spending far too much of my time trying to shake up those with toxic faith and religion addiction."

"I've never heard of toxic faith," I replied.

"Faith becomes sick," Grace answered, "when you worship the idols that dominate and oppress; emotions, ideas, needs, and wishes, rather than the God who is distinct but not separate from how you feel, think, or imagine.

"When you create God out of your needs and desires and then worship the god you expect to fulfill both, your faith becomes warped. Healthy spirituality lets God be God in the reality of what is. Of course, when you are young, it's understandable to approach God out of your need for a comfortable life, but as you grow older you hopefully discover that a healthy and loving relationship cannot be based only on what the other can do and be for you. A healthy relationship must let the other be who they are, as they are, not as you merely wish them to be.

"Actually, John," Grace continued, "your faith became sick when you expected God to take away the pain of your brother Paul's death, and addictive when you thought God would reward you for your hard work by giving you only good feelings about yourself.

"There is really no such a thing as prayer, anyway, John," Grace said. "Prayer is a relationship, not an object. Prayer becomes toxic, however, when people think that by doing certain things they can get more of God or even worse, power over God. God can't help but give all that God is, to all, all the time. No matter what you do you can't get any more of God tomorrow than you have today.

"After all, God doesn't dole out bits and pieces of God to those who flawlessly perform all their religious practices, who go to church more often than their neighbor, who are stuck in shame, guilt, inferiority, or inadequacy, or who merely want to feel better. You may, of course, learn to open yourself more to the God who is by purging your faith of the little gods you worship out of need and fear, but you can't get any more of the Presence of God than you've already got.

"Toxic prayer, however, is more than just a dangerous overemphasis on the things you do in prayer. It is also the destructive idea that through the rituals you perform you can manipulate God.

"If you come to this Chapel of Prayer, John," Grace concluded "to hide from the storms of life or to proclaim a faith in a magical god whose only task is to increase your bottom line of profit, power, position, pleasure, or prestige, then your prayer is sick and your god toxic. A god you can control is not a god at all."

"How, Grace," I asked, "do I find the Present God, the God free of my needs and expectations?"

"You don't have to search for God," Grace answered, "because God has already found you. What you must do is let go of your passions, ideas, wishes, and expectations, the little gods you worship for what they will do for you, and accept the Presence of a God who continually gifts you with the courage to face reality, your own and God's."

"Will you teach me, Grace," I asked, "to let go of the gods of my making so that I can let be the God that is making me?"

"That is precisely my task," Grace answered. "I've been about the business of gracing all creation with the gifts of God long before human beings ever processed a thought through their central nervous systems. Let me tell you a story that may help you put down the little gods that burden your life with so much suffering and misery.

"Two of your fellow Passionate Monks, John, were walking one very rainy day from one Monastery to another. As they walked they discussed great and marvelous philosophical and theological issues; ideas, I might add, that often hide as much of God as they reveal.

"During the course of their journey the Monks came to a crossroads which had become flooded into a large puddle that blocked their path. Standing on the edge of the puddle was a finely dressed woman in a long gown. The Missionary Monk, Richard, went over to the woman and offered to carry her through the water. The woman was very appreciative and climbed upon his back. When Richard reached the other side of the puddle he put the woman down, said good-bye and continued his journey with his fellow Monk, Ernest.

"That evening, after Richard and Ernest had settled into the Monastery, they sat together in the common room continuing their high-minded conversation. During the course of their discussion, however, Ernest, angry and upset by what he had seen Richard do on the journey, finally confronted his friend.

"'Richard,' he said, 'how could you carry that woman on your back in public? You know as well as I do that Monks aren't supposed to have anything to do with women. Yet you allowed that woman to climb on your back for all to see. Weren't you at all concerned with what others might think if they saw you? Your actions not only disgraced me but our entire Order of Monks,' Ernest practically yelled. 'What do you have to say to justify your behavior?'

"Richard sat back in his chair for a moment of reflection and quietly responded, 'Ernest, I put the woman down over five hours ago, why can't you?'[5]

"Now, don't misunderstand me here, John," Grace continued. "I did not tell you this story to discourage healthy relationships with the opposite sex but rather to encourage you to let go of your life as you live it, to put down your need to control the future so that you can embrace the world freely.

"You must stop lying to yourself, John, about the god you believe in and believe in the God who believes in you. You, John, must move from depending on God to protect you from life's reality, to protecting God from your fears and needs. After all, only the God of all creation can help you carry reality."

"But, Grace," I asked, "which little god does God want me to put down today?"

"You have so many I don't know where to begin," Grace answered. "Yours will be a lifetime of putting down the lying gods that you have spent a lifetime picking up. If the god you worship grows out of your fear of life's difficulties then your faith is sick and your god toxic. If your god is a god who rewards you with success for working hard then your god does not exist anywhere else but in your ambition and need to please. You must remember that your personal images of God often arise out of your unconscious, out of the inner crowd that so easily motivates and manipulates you, as well as out of what society deems holy and acceptable.

"In order to put down the gods of your own making you must look within yourself to see who it is that is doing the image-making: fear, ambition or anger. The gods you worship are legion because you make them out of your chattering inner passions, wishes, and emotions. To be present to the one God who is eternally present to you, you must first identify who you need God to be for you at the moment and let that god go. Only when you recognize that God is distinct from but not separate from your thoughts and feelings, desires and senses can God be free to be the freedom that sets all creation free.

"Prayer," Grace continued, "is a process not a product, a letting go of the little gods of fleeting feelings, passing thoughts and limiting desires so that you can then contemplate the God who is contemplating you. The more you pray honestly, John, the more you'll denounce the gods you need to worship for your sake and affirm the God that is eternally challenging and encouraging you.

"It is time now, John," Grace concluded "for you to pray good-bye to the magical gods you've carved so well out of fear and ambition, the deceiver who promises to take away the pain and make life blissfully happy, the idol that judges harshly those who do not worship as you think they ought and the god of power who doles out positions of prestige.

"You may, at times, of course, anxiously miss the gods of the quick and easy fix, who momentarily fill up the lonely spaces of life with comfort and security, but you must say good-bye anyway. These gods are, after all, much too small."

"I'd long forgotten, Grace," I said, finally speaking up, "how freeing a conversation with you could be. I'm thankful that Aquinas led me back to Prayer's sanctuary."

"This place exists for only one purpose," Grace said firmly, "and that is for freedom's sake. This sanctuary is the space where you and your fellow believers can share the common story of prayer:

"The cry of my anguish went up to God,
'Lord, take away my pain!

The shadow that darkens the world
    you have made;
The close coiling chain
That strangles the heart: the burden
    that weighs
On the wings that soar—
Lord, take away the pain from the
    world you have made
That it and I may love you the more!'

Then answered the Lord to the cry of
    the world,
'Shall I take away pain,
And with it the power of the soul to
    endure and thrive,
Made strong by strain?
Shall I take away compassion that
    knits heart to heart,
And sacrifice high?
Will you lose all your heroes that rise
    from the fire,
White brows to the sky?
Shall I take away love that redeems
    with a price,
And smiles with its loss?
Can you spare from your lives what
    would cling unto mine?
The Christ on the cross?' "[6]

John Powers

"Tell me now, John," Grace asked, "who God is for you today?"

In response to Grace's question I echoed the long-lost memory I hear resounding within me.

"Today I affirm God
as the life behind the living,
the activity behind all giving.

I affirm God as the Gift-giver,
who gives what God is and is what
God gives.

I affirm God as Creativity,
who continually makes life out of universal and personal chaos, out of
pain and pleasure, love and loss, life
and death.

I pray to be creative as God is creative,
to make life out of the mess I've got
and am
rather than out of what I wish would be.

I affirm God as Courage,
the mighty first and eternal risk-taker,
who dares create me free enough to
reject even divinity.

I pray to be brave enough
to believe in myself, others and God,
enough to live with failure, sin and
    vulnerability
and enough not to deny in the dark-
    ness what I've seen in the light.

I affirm God as contemplative
    Presence,
who is closer to me than I am to myself.

I pray every day that I may learn to
    contemplate the God who is con-
    templating me.

I affirm God as Compassion,
a kindly kin consciousness,
a power with and for life.

I pray for a spirit that is thicker than
    blood,
a spirit of kinship with all creation,
especially with the weak and the strong
within and around me.

I affirm today the God
who works with what God's got,
a fearful yet gifted human being like me."

"The God that you affirm today, John," Grace said, "has been affirming you with the gifts of creativity, courage, compassion, and contemplative presence throughout your journey. This is precisely why I've joined you today in the Chapel of Prayer, to give you what God can't help but give and be God. I'm here to bless you with the resilient courage to get up when you fall down, to change your perspective when you are trapped by narrow ideas and to put down the gods of your own making. God is the courageous Presence that helps you go on precisely at the moment when you are absolutely convinced you can't."

"Grace," I said, "I have a rather specific question to ask about prayer. Can I still pray in petition, asking God to come to the aid of a hurting friend, a child in poverty, or to grant me the courage I need to go on?"

"Of course you can," Grace answered, "but remember your prayer of petition is more for your comfort than for God's information. God is already present precisely where you need God to be. The best you can do in prayer is hold your need or the names of those you love in your heart so that God can see them there and continue to do what, I've already said, God does best—give fuller and fuller life.

"Remember now, John," Grace continued, "as you leave this Chapel of Prayer, that God continues the performance God began before the beginning. As God, the great Storyteller spun out of the void the creative world and activity so God continues to spin creation in and through you today.

"In every moment, God is weaving together your many feelings, thoughts, needs, and passions, recollecting and recreating your heart and soul. Unlike multiminded human beings, God's purpose is singular, to be one with the human heart, to gather together your shattered feelings, scattered thoughts, frail senses, and overwhelming passions into harmony. As God works in recollecting you, John, work with God by living a prayerful life-style wherever you go."

As I stood to leave the Chapel Grace asked, "Where would you like me to guide you today, young priest?"

"Well, Grace," I said, "that's, of course, always up to you, but I happen to know Richard, the Passionate Monk you mentioned in your earlier story about letting go. We've been friends for some twenty years. Richard is a wise Missionary Priest who has ministered for over ten years in the Valley of Poverty many miles south of the City of Chaos in a country called Honduras. Its Poverty has taught Richard that to travel far you must travel light. Since Richard has graciously invited me to visit with him in the Valley of Poverty during the upcoming holiday, I've decided to journey to Honduras."

"The Have-Nots have an important story to tell the Haves," Grace said, "so remain a listener and learner during your pilgrimage, John."

Suddenly the Chapel door flew open and Richard stood in the frame. "Come on, John," he said, as he pointed to the sacred saying on the wall, rephrasing as he read aloud, "God works with the mess God's got."

VALLEY OF POVERTY

As Richard, the Passionate Missionary, and I climbed into the Valley of Poverty only an hour outside the capital city of Tegucigalpa, Honduras, we shared, as friends often do, bits and pieces of our stories. Having already ministered for three years in an orphanage in Mexico, Richard was now involved in the building of a new home for the orphans of Honduras.

Although Richard's heart had cracked many times over at the sight of destitute and sick children, it seemed to have been reinforced by Grace's promised presence. It was not scars of cynicism that wrapped round Richard's heart but rather a binding compassion that gave him a physical capacity I could only admire. Compassion gave Richard eyes to see in the dark, back alleys of society and the strength of heart to be a light in the tunnel of deprivation.

Richard's ministry was not with the mainstream of society but with those children on the far edge, the homeless street hustlers, those given up by father or mother, and babies suffering from AIDS. Richard put his heart, soul, and back into the building of a home for the thrown away children.

"Isn't happiness enough, John?" Richard asked as we drove the half-tarred, rugged rocked road into the coarse dry valley. "It's those who are never satisfied with the enough they already have who directly deprive others of the enough they desperately need.

"According to Oxfam America," Richard continued, "we live in a world where 800 million people endure absolute poverty while 60,000 die of hunger every day, 40,000 of whom are children. Every minute of every day 30 children die because they don't have enough food or because they can't get the inexpensive vaccines that will help keep them alive, while in the very same minute the world absorbs almost $1.7 million in public funds for military budgets.

"Did you know, John," Richard asked, "that 73 percent of the world's population lives with extreme or high misery? That according to the recent Population Crisis Committee's Index some 4 billion people suffer from either the lack of clean water, insufficient daily calorie intake, lower life expectancy, are deprived of political freedom and civil rights, or all of the above? Obviously there's both an abundance of deprivation in this world as well as a poverty of realistic concern and compassion.

"You and I, John," Richard continued, "come from the social background of the United States, where, it may surprise you to discover, households with yearly incomes of less than $10,000 give almost twice as much (5.5 percent) of that income to charity than do those earning $100,000 a year (2.9 percent).

"We live in an economically abundant but spiritually deprived world, where the haves can easily decide what they wish to eat next week or month while the have-nots have to worry about what they will eat today, where power is determined to a large extent by just how far into the future you can plan your menu.

"The haves are terrified of sharing the power to control the future with the have-nots. For many a have, money is merely a power tool to secure a comfortable tomorrow where wants can easily slip into necessities."

When I eventually asked Richard what he tries to do for the children of his growing orphanage and for the babies in the AIDS hospice, he replied:

"First we provide food and medical care so that the children can survive long enough to have a chance to thrive through the educational opportunities we offer. We also pray a lot because ministry makes no sense without it. After all, religion that does not feed the children has no soul, while the soul that does not pray is lost. A spirituality that does not seek justice is not healthy or Christian.

"Each night," Richard continued, "I whisper to the children the story of a compassionate man named Jesus who, although he may not physically reach in to deprive them of their poverty, is, however, always present in their sleeping and playing, running and weeping. It is Christ who lives in this poor valley."

"And what do you pray for the most?" I asked.

"Oh, I don't pray for things," Richard answered, "although we have a desperate need for food and fuel, diapers and clothes. Instead I hold the children in my arms in play and in sickness and let God do what God has promised: love them.

"I pray for the children who just can't make up their minds which pair of shoes to wear to school and for those who have only one pair and those are too big or too small.

"I pray for those who pray for an expensive toy at Christmas and for those who haven't got a prayer.

"I pray for the children who after divorce can't decide which parent they want to live with and for those little ones whose parents have left them on the street.

"I pray for those who forget their lunch money and for those who have no lunch, for those who stick lollipops in their hair and for those whose lice-infested hair must be lopped off.

"I pray for the children who play in puddles and those who wash in sewers, for those who make a fuss about going to bed and for those who have no bed to fuss over.

"I pray for those suffering from anorexia and bulimia and for those who have no choice but to eat out of the garbage.

"I pray for the little boy who wants a toy gun and for the little girl who must sleep with the sound of gunfire because little boys become big boys with big toys.

"I pray for the children who get picked on at school and the children who have no school to go to, for those who lay awake at night listening to their parents fight and for those who wish they could remember what their parents looked like, for those who cry that they will just die if they don't get a new toy or pair of Levi's and for those who do just die.

"I pray for the children who have never been taught to pray and for those who pray for the strength to survive today.

"I pray and then I get off my knees to do the impossible, try to answer my own prayer."

As Richard shared his prayer and wealth of information and insight into the unjust distribution of the world's goods, we passed through the gates of the orphanage. On a tree near the entrance was nailed a homemade sign which read: OUR LITTLE BROTHERS AND SISTERS.

I had no idea the day I joined the children in their Valley of Poverty that I would become the student and they, the poor and powerless, my mentors. Among the deprived, however, it is often those who have thrived through the greatest misery who are given the power to teach.

The lessons began in earnest as the children took my hand and led me into the heart of their playing, singing, dancing, and eating. It was December 31st and the children were ready for a New Year's celebration.

After lifting perhaps every one of the eighty some children on my back for a ride, and rumbling in the dirt with the boys who wanted to bring me down to size, I danced around a large fire, sang songs and shot off firecrackers. We ended the evening's activities with a celebration of the Lord's meal of simple bread and wine in a barn.

As the children continued their dancing to popular American rock music deep into New Year's morning I crawled my way to a much too short top bunk bed only to lay awake reflecting on the happenings of the day.

It was children on the edge who challenged me to exchange the passion of self-centered pleasures for a compassionate concern, who taught me that the only way I can thrive in life rather than merely endure or survive through life is if I accept an essential "usness," a kinship with others.

The children reminded me once again that the only justification for going within yourself is to go outside yourself, that Therapy Bridge does not merely take you into the more comfortable country of selfishness but rather carries you into the heartland of responsibility.

I learned that the least of all the brethren, the very enemy himself, the poorest of all the poor is not outside myself but rather within me. It is that coldness of heart that turns others into objects to be dominated for my security.

I realized that once having faced my inner fears, ambitions, and greed in therapy I was not only free to walk out into the brightness of the day but responsible to share that glaring freedom with others. After all is said and done you can only become free if you set others free, grow strong and sane if you share power, and become complete in yourself if you build community.

"Personal growth," I recalled Richard saying as we trekked into the Valley, "cannot be a substitute for political action. Becoming too focused on the inner community not only isolates us from others but can blind us to the very social conditions that cause and perpetuate poverty and pain in the outer community.

"The truest goal of religion and personal growth, after all, is not self-adulation, but rather inspired and inspiring action that helps solve some of the world's most complex problems.

"From personal experience," Richard continued, "I confess that by trying to live in solidarity with the poor and powerless I've learned to live in greater solidarity with my own imperfections and vulnerabilities. By accepting my weakness I have set free my strength to work for social and political change.

"It's my flawedness that has taught me to live as an ally with the feelings and thoughts and passions that rage on the inner stage and as kin to all that moves about me, acting always to make the world a better place to live in."

Still covered from head to toe with dirt I drifted off to sleep that New Year's night realizing how tightly I was bound to Richard, the children, and the earth.

Rising early the next morning, I went to sit in the open air with what passed as a cup of coffee. The eighty degree wind blew the dry brown earth into the air, leaving a mist of dust hanging quietly in the shafts of bright sunlight. It was a glorious morning to be soaked in the lessons children have a way of spilling all over you.

After a few minutes of sitting alone I noticed that Santos (translated to mean holy), a fifteen-year-old boy recently taken from a hospital bed to spend what could be the last days of his life with the other children, was also up and about, wandering along the edge of an uneven soccer field the children practically lived in.

When Santos saw me sitting alone he made a roundabout trip my way, walking with the caution of one whose stomach was bloated by a liver disease caused by his grandfather's misuse of dangerous pesticides in the family garden. Santos's legs were almost fleshless bone while his skin had turned a dark diseased yellow. I was again saddened by the fact that I spoke no Spanish, and he no English, as Santos finally eased his frail body next to me on the picnic bench.

Having recognized each other with a quick connecting glance we sat in silence. After only a few minutes, however, Santos did something that not only took my breath away, but put it back again. With cautious grace, Santos gently lifted his arm around my shoulder. By far Santos carried the heavier burden, but so too did he have the lightest touch.

At that moment kinship became a concrete reality, a grace that saved me from my own indifference to the pain of others. In the lightness of an instant I realized, then, that not only were Santos and I connected by the thickness of the spirit but that, perhaps on an even deeper level, that I was Santos and Santos was me; that what I shared with him I gave myself and what I took from him I stole from myself. Santos, I realized, was my brother, one with me rather than one of them. Or could it be that it was I who was one of them? Grace only knows.

Although not related by family bloodline we shared a kin consciousness, a brotherly concern; feeling each other's pain, intuiting each other's dreams while seeing the world through each other's eyes for just long enough to permanently change my perspective.

When two or three are gathered anywhere together there is Grace, joining heart to heart. Santos's heartbeat, however, was slow and costly, sending fear flowing through my veins.

In a shiver of shared pain the touch of Santos's arm on my back not only brought tears of sentiment to my eyes but transported me out of a self-imposed self-centeredness, shattering any sense of inequality.

No longer could I look at another human being as he or she passed by on television or right in front of me, and say what is so often easily and callously said, "He's one of them." Through one human touch Santos and I communicated, becoming a kind of kin amid the poor and broken.

In my powerlessness I felt a strong and binding spirit I'd only rarely felt before, a graceful gravity that pulls and pushes us together whether we like it or not.

I felt honored to be a part of Santos's family, one among the homeless.

KINGDOM OF KINSHIP

What Santos said, Grace translated. "When you deprive others of their just due you deprive yourself; you fall from grace. When you oppress others you degrade yourself, abandoning your humanity. You become the inferior of every person you step on in order to become king of the mountain of prestige, position, power, pleasure and pennies.

"To affirm another, however, is to confirm your own dignity. What you do to the least of your brothers and sisters you do unto yourself. If you lift up you are raised. If you build community outside yourself, unity is formed within as well."

With only a touch, Santos transported me from the world of arrogance and indifference, where there are so-called first, second, third or even fourth worlders into the Kingdom of Kinship where the power-to-be-with-and-for-others is far stronger than power-over can ever be.

"Power," Santos reminded me, and Grace rendered "can be used as a hammer that sees everything as a problem to be nailed into place or as a key that unlocks the door that imprisons the haves in indifference and the have-nots in poverty. Power is what you do with it.

"It may be only a truism, but it may also be true, that to the extent you measure your self-worth by how much power over others you have, are you the weakest of all. To the degree you are addicted to a power-over mentality, which is, of course, motivated always by fear and insecurity, will others become a threat and you a tyrant. The oppressor is always the one with the most fear, fear that they are just like everyone else. The truly powerful are those wise enough to know that they most assuredly are.

"What you have is directly connected to what I cannot get," Santos said and Grace translated. "And if you think that hand outs to the have-nots will continue to gain you respect then you'd better think again. The have-nots may accept your humanitarian aid—after all the poor can't afford to be against charitable giving—still they would much prefer that you change the unjust social system upon which hand outs are built.

"When the poor closely examine the haves we see how often the generosity of benefactors is overshadowed by the greed of old tyrants desperately trying to keep their balance on top of a mountain of wants. We see men and women who believe that power is more important than service, things more valuable than people, laws stand above justice, some people are better than others, pleasure is more important than love, and who worship the belief that someone must lose so that they can win.

"It is not foreign aid that we need so much as opportunity, not a political-economic structure built on competition but one built on and building compassion and conversion. What we the have-nots demand is a radical change in the socioeconomic structure of the world, not the toxic charity that keeps us indentured in the service of the tyrant.

"Let me make an important point here, John," Santos said through Grace, "one that, although it should not be made too much of must still be recognized.

"Like the many multiminded haves who chase after even more, so too there are many have-nots who suffer under the same illusion that happiness is merely getting what you want. Poverty, after all, does not necessarily make for purity of intent.

"More commonly, however, the poor and powerless are driven by real needs, what is justly due them as creatures of the earth and not by mere wants for comfort and contentment sake."

"I know, Santos," I said, finally speaking up, "that there are far too many people whose only daily prayer seems to be;

> 'All hail, almighty Inc's and Ideologies,
> all powerful United Fruit, Coca-Cola,
> Baby Food Companies, Lumber and
> Mineral gods who may create the jobs
> but whose priorities are always
> profits over people, production over
>   process.
>
> We worship you all-knowing economic
>   systems
> communism, capitalism or whatever
>   variation is in power—
> you who slice the masses into social
>   classes
> while doling out protection, land or
>   profits
> to those with the biggest assets.'

"But what, Santos," I asked, "can I do to change the unjust socioeconomic and political world structure, with its unequal distribution of wealth and opportunity.

"I too feel a hint of guilt, and to be honest, an ounce of arrogant annoyance, every time I hear the frequently proclaimed statistic that 80 something percent of the natural resources of the world are used by only 20 something percent of the world's population. But what can I do?" I asked. "What can one person do?"

"Do what you can to put compassion where it isn't," Santos said and Grace repeated. "And then try the seemingly impossible, to stop human beings from crucifying each other and the earth.

"The least you can do, John, is stand in solidarity, in kinship with the crucified of today. You can, after all, change yourself by confronting your ignorance, bigotry and arrogant ways. You may not be responsible for ordering the world as it is but once aware you become responsible for what you see. You become obligated to unmask the evil that strings people into puppets.

"Evil," Santos continued, "has many masks but indifference is its most demonic. The moment you start taking off the mask of apathy, justice has a possibility, at least a fighting chance. The only way to fight evil is to fight indifference, to raise the level of awareness and consciousness in yourself and others. You must care enough to confront those who do not care. Only when you take off the mask of indifference can you discover that the face hidden behind all others is the face of God.

"It's not so much what you do anyway, John," Santos communicated, "whether you give money, time, or talent, care for those in your own backyard, open up opportunities for others, march or protest or even travel to work among the poor of this world, but that you do what you can, where you are, with what you have to build a kinship of compassion with those who have not.

"If each person cared, for example," Santos concluded, "for only those born on the same day they were born, the world would be tight with kinship."

The lessons of that bright New Year's morning continued as Santos then reached into his pocket, took out a neatly folded piece of paper and handed it to me. Although I wondered where he'd found the typed verse of English and why he'd carry it around with him, I read the words on the yellowing page:

> If you have only a few loaves and a
> few fish and so many are hungry...

John Powers

If there are only six jars of water and
    no one is happy with you . . .
If there is only one little mustard
    seed . . .
If the only way out is through
    Egypt . . .
If there are only a few stories and no
    titles or degrees . . .
If you have only a few friends and
    they're all asleep . . .
If you seem not to have a father in
    your darkest hour, and your mother
    wasn't there . . .
If all you have are a few words and a
    shred of hope . . .
Still, if the word of God is in you, you
    win!
Not for yourself, but for everyone.
Nothing is lost—not the coin nor the
    sheep nor Peter who denies, nor the
    Pharisee who comes to Christ in the
    night.
For the word of the Lord crumbles
    Jerusalem, Rome and Athens.
The word is not rhetoric, it is history.
It is within us—and all the while we
    kept thinking we needed something
    more.[7]

"Compassion," Santos said graciously, as he took the paper from my hand, "is the ability to see one's self in another, to enter into the very passion of another's life. It is not uncommon, however, for people to mistake compassion with pity, thinking that to commiserate with another or feel bad because they hurt is to be compassionate. Compassion, however, has little time for pity. Compassion means to enter into another's joys and sorrows, delights and hurts, to look at others with the eyes of kin consciousness. Compassion makes 'us' out of 'me.'

"The individualism of 'me,' is, after all, incompatible with healthy spirituality," Grace translated. "The task of religion is not, however, merely to create believers but more importantly to build a community of kin who work to make this world a better place for all to live in, believers or not.

"There is a story told," Santos continued, "about a newly elected President of a newly formed country that might be helpful here:

"The President of the new country decided that his first order of business should be to have a flag made to which the people could salute, so he went to a tailor to have a national flag designed and sewn.

"The poor tailor was as first pleased that the

President would ask him to design and sew the country's first flag but found the task increasingly disappointing as he sewed one flag after another only to have each design rejected by the state flag committee.

"Finally in utter frustration the tailor took a large white sheet off his bed, wrote one word on one side, another word on the other side and took it to the committee as his last attempt.

"The committee took one look at the sheeted flag and immediately accepted it. A large celebration was held to raise the new flag above the National Assembly building. A huge crowd gathered. When the flag was finally run up the pole a cry of glory roared from the crowd. As the flag cracked sharply in the breeze the words the tailor had scrawled were easy to read. On one side of the flag was written the word *US* and on the other side the word *THEM*.

"People of compassion," Santos continued, "*in*clude those that the self-righteous and insecure *ex*clude. No one is merely 'one of them' to someone of compassion. A compassionate person has respect for the essential dignity of human beings, affirms others for who they are, not for what they can do, shares what goods they have so others can survive, and creates opportunities and possibilities so that others can thrive.

"Of course," Santos graciously continued, human beings learn best to be compassionate in an atmosphere of justice. When you receive no more than your just due, thankfulness urges you to return in kind. We are, after all, connected by something deeper and richer than blood, the spirit of a compassionate God who gives us more than enough compassion than we need while asking us to share more than we think we have."

Before I left the orphanage only a week into the New Year to return to the Monastery of Passion I sought out Santos out to say what I thought would be a last good-bye. Since I knew from the Missionary, Richard, that Santos was expected to die from his illness very soon, I wanted to put my arm on his shoulder.

After searching for some time without success among the children and in the woods around the soccer field I finally came upon Santos rolled into a fetal position on a bunk bed at the far end of a dormitory room.

As I sat on the edge of the bunk to simply be with him for a few minutes as he slept I heard the ever present whisper of Grace interpret the silence.

"One thing you will never hear a compassionate person say, after someone has passed by is, 'There but for the grace of God go I.' Nonsense! I don't make the distinctions you humans do, picking and choosing who I'll travel with and who I won't. I journey with everyone without distinction. No one is deprived of my full presence. It's part of the human inheritance. God gives all to all in graceful measure.

"The problem among you humans," Grace concluded, "is that far too many of you arrogantly believe that history, power, or position has anointed you with the authority to decide who is deserving of God's grace and life's opportunities and who isn't.

"People of compassion, however, know that 'There in the grace of God we go'—that if you travel together you can go as far as the Kingdom of Kinship."

As I sat on the edge of Santos's bunk listening to his soft breathing my throat constricted and my tear ducts opened to fill the lower rims of my eyes. I stared for a time at the floor wondering what would happen to this graced and dying child.

Eventually shifting my focus from my shoes back to Santos's face I was surprised to find him not only staring intently at me but also laughing. Of all things, Santos was laughing.

Perhaps the air did not burst forth from

Santos's frail lungs at 70 miles an hour, as I've heard can be the speed of a belly laugh—his was lighter, traveling at perhaps only 30 to 40 miles per hour—but he laughed nonetheless. Santos's stomach may have been distended with disease but his heart was strong enough to laugh.

I wondered as I embraced Santos what we were laughing at. Perhaps we laughed at the paradoxical absurdities of life, that you can learn more about living from the dying, more about having enough from those who have too little than from those who have too much, more about strength from the weak than from those who seem to have control, more about power from the powerless than from those who dominate, more from loss of love than from love alone, and more from a human touch than from a library of books.

Perhaps, I thought, the intention of life, after all, is that we actually enjoy life, giving ourselves permission to laugh, at least as often as life requires we cry.

COMING HOME

As I climbed aboard the jet that would return me to the Mountain of Choice in Imagi Nation, I realized how much homework I had to do to integrate the lessons life had taught as I walked, played, cried, worshiped, ate, and laughed with my little brothers and sisters in the Valley of Poverty.

One child's face after another flashed across my mind's sky as I flew both physically and emotionally home. I was so moved by the children, especially by Santos's capacity to laugh amid the pain, that even when I looked out the window of the jet to see that we were flying directly over the Isle of Ignorance, I felt little desire to return to that prison of conscience. I cannot say that I will always want to face the truth that life offers or learn what Grace has to teach, but I do believe that awareness is forever healthier and holier than ignorance.

Looking, then, off to the horizon, far beyond the Isle of Ignorance, Fantasy Land, the Sea of Love and Loss, and the Land of Pain, I saw once again the beautifully high and dangerous peaks of the Mountain of Choice. I was on my way home, where I fit in not because of what I had but precisely because of my limitations, because of what I lacked.

While staring deep into myself the voice of the elderly and eloquent woman sitting next to me interrupted my reverie.

"So you've heard the sound of salvation in the laughter of a dying boy. No matter what the language, laughter sounds the same, doesn't it?"

"Grace," I said gladly, "you're just the one I wanted to talk to. Funny how you seem to be everywhere, conveniently showing up just when I need to talk."

"To rephrase an old gag line," Grace answered, "funny is relative and some relatives are funnier than others. I haven't gone any-where," she continued. "We are kin, bound together by the thick humor of the spirit. I've been with you all the while, leading you home to the Temple of Laughter, where honest humor and perspective reign hand in hand.

"As you climbed out of the Valley of Poverty in the Kingdom of Kinship Santos did indeed give you a wondrous going-home present, and to think he gave you the gift of laughter free of charge.

"Hold tight to this paradoxical gift, however, John, the perspective that reminds you that it is precisely your imperfection and confusion that is funny, for only with laughter can you travel through the Land of Pain or Fantasy, visit the Valley of Poverty, know the streets of Success City or cross the Bridge of Therapy on your way home to yourself."

"I've often thought that life was a joke," I answered smartly.

"You're absolutely correct," Grace answered. "Life commonly seems to be a silly joke, unfair, ridiculous, unkind and cruel, but tragic, never! Only holy fools get the punchline, however, finding meaning amid the absurdity of life, in the measure of difference between how things are and how you want or think they ought to be."

"Upon reflection, Grace," I continued, "I've come to realize and accept more fully that I am singularly imperfect, most laughable and foolish when I try to be perfectly in control, right, in charge, and on top of the world, rather than living peacefully in it."

"A healthy sense of humor," Grace said, "is a vital sign that God's heart beats in your heart,

John, that comedy is inevitable, while tragedy is optional. After all, laughter is what the soul of every humor being is made of."

"Here, Grace," I said as I reached for my wallet, "let me read you a poem that was written by a mutual friend of ours when I was ordained a Catholic Priest some years ago." After cautiously unfolding the yellowing gift I read it aloud:

" 'The soul of a man—that awe-inspiring miracle that laughs gleefully in captivity—can be described only one way; as the joyful dance. It leaps merrily through the labyrinth of the heart; fearless in the presence of the heart's terror, placid in the midst of the heart's despair. It thrills when the heart rejoices, and nearly expires with ecstasy when the heart loves. The soul of a man, laughing freely, dances lightly in the veiled presence of Mystery.' "

"Since the best friends," Grace said, "are those who teach you to laugh at yourself, you can be sure that whoever wrote that poem is a soul-friend. The author of that piece understands that a sense of humor is an innate and essential human quality that can help create a positive future for the human family. Only a holy foolish 'humor being' could know that the soul is made of the kind of wholesome laughter that blesses you with the divine perspective necessary to live with the pain of life."

"The author of the poem is Richard," I answered, "the Passionate Missionary in your earlier story about letting go and who I just visited in the Valley of Poverty."

"I know Richard quite well," Grace said. "In fact, John, while you were recently playing with the children at the orphanage, Richard and I were having a long conversation about his dream to go to medical school so that he can be more effective in his ministry among the poor.

"It's people like Richard who make my graceful work a lot easier. He's one Christian believer who knows that laughter is not just a survival tool but a necessity, a nightlight in the darkness, a bridge that leads from pain to possibility.

"However, our missionary friend," Grace continued, "is an exception among the human family not the rule. For far too many, laughter isn't made so much of soul for the building up of strength and kinship as it's made of anger and fear. Aggressive humor, however, is artificial, and cruel, doing little more than mocking or shaming others.

"Sad to say, I see far more snickers of denial, sneers of bigotry or sarcastic grins of arrogance than I hear laughs that come from the heart and soul. Those who use laughter to mask their true feelings, escaping reality rather than honestly facing it, give humor a bad name.

"Did you know," Grace asked, "that there are only three ways of living with reality, John? You can either fight what is, thinking that you can actually dominate or subdue reality to suit yourself; you can take flight from what is by living in the Land of Fantasy while wearing a mask of pretense; or you can face the chaos of life with a divinely universal and comic perspective. Only those who can play with reality can learn to laugh at the pain it offers."

"Learning to laugh," I said, "at the pain of life is a difficult concept to accept, Grace. It seems almost impossible."

"Nothing is impossible, John," Grace answered, "if you do what you can, where you are with the gifts you already have, and then laugh soulfully at your inability to do any more without the amusing grace of God."

"Funny," I said with a slight smile.

"I know from infinite experience," Grace continued, "that the reality of pain and poverty, death and failure, is not funny in a ha ha sort of way but is rather funny-odd. Reality seems strangely foreign to human beings because it never is as you think it ought to be, because you must live in a world you did not create and don't often like.

"If all you do, however, is wait for the world to become less threatening or strive to avoid all pain, you will miss the many absurd but blessed opportunities for creative, courageous, compassionate, contemplative, and comic living that are rolling by you at breakneck speed.

"To enjoy life you must enlarge your frame of reference from the personal and serious to the unlimited and comic. Honest humor, by violating the rational order of what is supposed to be, helps you look at life through God's eyes, developing a cosmic perspective that transforms your private sufferings into common comedy. There would be no comedians in this life or the next if there were no sorrows and pain. Isn't life, after all, much too important to be taken too seriously?

"As I've said over and over again to any who would listen," Grace continued, "if you can laugh at it you can live with it, especially if you can laugh at yourself. When you can laugh at your own inconsistency you may not only make it more enjoyable for others to live with you, but you may also be giving them the very example they need to learn to laugh at and live with their pains and vulnerabilities, hurts and disappointments.

"When you look at yourself through the universal yet intimate eyes of God you cannot help but see how absurdly narrow the human perspective often is, how controlled and dominated you are by a multitude of emotions, thoughts, needs, desires, and wishes, how easily habituated and conditioned you become to the small doses of pleasure, power, and prestige that society packages and how ridiculous it is to spend the first half of life anxiously preparing for the second half of life and then spend the second half haunted by memories and regrets from the first half.

"When you look at yourself through the eyes of God," Grace concluded, "it's much easier to let the 185 billion bits of information that can flow through your central nervous system in the course of seventy years pass by without hitching your worth and identity to any few pieces that seem pressing."

"It's amazing, Grace," I said, finally speaking up, "but as you spoke about looking at life through the eyes of God a few bits in my central nervous system seemed to recycle themselves into a memory.

"I recall another dying child," I continued, "beside Santos, who never lost a divine perspective, who was able to laugh amid the cruelest pain. His name was Paul Joseph.

"Because in innocence Paul's heart remained one with God's heart, he was able through all the physical pain to laugh with a laugh so infectious that it would sweep easily around the family dinner table causing uproarious belly laughs. Night after night, Paul held forth from the high chair of humor, tossing food and making faces. It was Paul's laughter that helped my parents, brothers, sisters and I live with the pain of watching death inch closer and closer."

"Death," Grace responded, "has only one lesson for human beings, to teach you to laugh at and enjoy the unintended, uncontrollable, inevitable, unexplainable, and idiotic foolishness of life."

"But how, Grace," I asked, "can I learn to laugh at death?"

"By taking your present ministry and work in life seriously but not your illusions of security or permanence. These you can find only in the arms of God.

"Did you know," Grace asked, "that according to one of your great playwrights, even Lazarus, a soul-friend of Jesus, was able to laugh in the face of mortality, and that was after he died? You recall the scene, don't you John, when Jesus was standing outside of Lazarus' tomb, calling out 'Lazarus, come out, come out wherever you are' or something like that?"

"Yes," I said, "I remember that Jesus not only cried at the death of Lazarus but that through love was able to raise his friend from the tomb."

"Well, in a Eugene O'Neill play," Grace continued, "Lazarus comes forth from the tomb, faces family, friends and Jesus and then does something so holy, human and unexpected that it takes the remainder of the play to explain it."

"What did Lazarus do?" I asked.

"Why it's the title of the play," Grace answered. "*Lazarus Laughed,* because he claimed to have heard the heart of Jesus laughing in his heart.

"The only way you can die laughing, John, is to live laughing and the only way you can live laughing is to die to the reality you think ought to be and accept the chaotic, free and often painful reality that is. Only when you accept your own absurd and haunting past can you rise up into the future. Tomorrow can be better than today, even the eternal tomorrow found in death, but only if you learn to accept and laugh at yesterday.

"Only a creative person, however, can learn to laugh at their fears, mistakes, losses, feelings, thoughts and the hurtful happenings of life,"

Grace said. "It is, after all, only those who laugh at themselves who can live well with themselves and others.

"Of course, if you can't seem to find anything about yourself or life to laugh at just remember that the average person, living some seventy-four years will spend seven of those years in the bathroom.

"You can't tell me that reality isn't funny," Grace concluded. "Laughter, or as I like to call it 'consecrated frivolity' is one of God's most durable gifts."

"I must confess, Grace," I said, "that I don't know many preachers who preach or churches that practice the spiritual attitude of consecrated frivolity."

"That's because," Grace answered, "when Christianity becomes the parade ground for the long-faced judgmental, militant believer to march, there's little room for the playground of the child. I know Faith personally and can assure you that she has the openness, resiliency, and flexibility of a child.

"Religion that excludes laughter," Grace continued, "is dead. The whole point of life and history is peace and laughter, isn't it? It's joyful laughter, not wailing and gnashing of teeth, that God wills for humor beings."

"Yes, but," I said, "there's the cross."

"You're absolutely right," Grace responded. "The crucifieds cannot be denied. The real question that must be asked and answered, however, John, is who is the crossmaker.

"In the solemn procession of the cross it's all too easy to forget that even Jesus Christ blessed laughter when he proclaimed that the very purpose of his preaching was so that 'my joy may be in you and your joy may be complete' (John 15:11).

"Religion," Grace continued, "is more about laughter and jubilation than crying and desperation. It's more about healing the hurts, loving those who hate you, seeing through eyes of faith, including the excluded, and admitting when you are wrong, while remaining spontaneously open before others. A holy sense of humor can help you do all this and more. It can help you enjoy the life that is yours, because that's what God wants for you. Religion, after all," Grace concluded, "is all about listening for the laughter of God in the unintended realities of life."

As the jet began to descend from the heights of my imagination Grace finished her remarks about "humor beings" and God by asking if I had any plans upon my return home. When I told her that I was thinking of writing another book, this one a witness to the radiance of my own discoveries she said:

"Isn't that what a priest is anyway, a story-teller? I've always found, of course, that the best storytellers are first and foremost careful story-listeners and therefore natural therapists. Only good listeners become truth-tellers.

"The most creative Priests and preachers I've ever worked with through inspiration," Grace continued, "have been those who trust the spir-ited imagination to lead the way, who look for God's story written between the lines of the human story.

"Stories, after all, build community both in psyche and society. When you listen to the sto-ries your emotions have to tell, the inner family is togethered a bit more closely. When you hear the story of a poor boy or a struggling single mother on welfare you become one with them in the telling. Storytelling and listening create community.

"Tell me though, John," Grace asked, "why do you want to work in what is for many an author a difficult and humbling profession?"

"Well, Grace," I answered, "as usual my motives are mixed. I believe I am motivated by 30 percent passion, 40 percent stupidity, 50 percent ego and 60 percent the fear of mathematics. I tell stories because I enjoy the intuitive and analytical process of writing, and because I'm an unfinished, incomplete, and imperfect human being. I tell stories because I don't have all the answers, because I can't control the future.

"Reading and writing, storytelling and listening," I concluded, "are prayer for me, connecting me with the creative force of God that continues to bring order out of chaos. The temporary order I synthesize out of the inner and outer chaos of my life may be only partial at best, momentary at most, but in prayer the ultimate connection with God lingers."

"Then write, John," Grace said, "about only the realities you have faced, taken by the neck, wrestled, played with, and laughed at. The task of the writer, after all, is not so much to perfect art as it is to perfect life. Good writers author themselves through their storytelling, hoping that the tales they tell will help them carry some of their pain. Whatever you do, John, do what you love and you can be sure that laughter will follow."

As Grace stood to disembark she leaned over, looked intently at me once again, and whispered ever so memorably:

"When you need me, John, to help you live with your own frailty, vulnerability and inconsistency, with the cruelest of life's pains or with the silly seriousness of some situation, laugh and I'll be with you.

"Of course, I can always be found in the Temple of Laughter located in the center of the City of Chaos in the Land of Pain on the corners of Awe Avenue and Surprise Street. Come for a visit and I'll give you a few suggestions on how you can find more joy in life."

TEMPLE OF LAUGHTER

Although I traveled regularly through the Land of my Pain and the pain of others it was some five or six years before I decided to take Grace up on her invitation to stop for a visit at the Temple of Laughter.

Of course, while I may not have gone out of my way to visit Grace during these years, she continued to travel with me, especially as I approached and began to break through what is now infamously called mid-life.

Grace was also very obvious in Santos's life as well during this stretch of years. He was brought to the United States by a group of compassionate people who not only raised the necessary $150,000 for surgery, but were able to return him to a healthier life among his kin in Honduras.

It was also during these years that my younger brother Peter and his wife Cindy birthed their first child, a boy they would choose to name Paul Joseph.

Although I often thought of visiting Grace during these breakthrough years and I easily remembered the address of the Temple, I was unsure where Awe Avenue and Surprise Street intersected in the City of Chaos. Since I knew, however, that according to the Yearbook of American and Canadian Churches, there were in my homeland approximately 346,102 Houses of Worship; 315,810 of which were Protestant, 23,561 Catholic, 3,416 Jewish, 1,662 of Eastern Religious persuasion and 100 Buddhist, I decided to simply take my chances and enter the first House of Worship I came upon.

It did not take me long to find the Temple of Laughter, however, for just around the corner from where I was walking was a church that had the following words etched above the door-frame: HONEST LAUGHTER IS THE SHORTEST DISTANCE BETWEEN YOU AND GOD.

I entered the brightly sunlit circular church to find Grace sitting quietly in the back of the worship hall while a small group of men, women and children were warmly conversing and laughing near the altar in front.

"Welcome, John, I was expecting you." Grace said.

"You're always expecting me," I said in

response.

"Isn't this a beautiful place to worship?" Grace asked, without waiting for a reply. "Did you know," she continued "that this Temple of Laughter was built by Faith? She's a personal friend of mine whose perspective on the future is eternally but realistically optimistic. And isn't the news wonderful?" she asked, as she pointed to the gathered people standing by the altar.

"What news is that?" I asked.

"Why the news," she answered, "about the increase in the average laugh expectancy in life recorded today at 410,078 for a person living seventy-four years of life."

"Is it the number of laughs in a lifetime that makes you happy?" I foolishly asked.

"Of course not," she answered. "What's important is the quality of the laugh. Of course, to determine quality you must look for the source of the laugh. If laughter comes from an honest heart it's soul-enhancing and can help heal emotional, relational, spiritual, and even physical dis-ease. However, if laughter roars up out of aggression, shame, or low self-esteem, it can only be destructive."

"Is everyone welcomed to worship in this Temple?" I asked.

"Oh, yes," Grace said, "we welcome all inner

and outer characters, especially the cynics, shamers and mockers with the hope that they too will learn to convert hostile passion into blessed laughter.

"Look again, John," Grace continued, "at the holy fools surrounding the altar. They are no different than you, except to say that their perspective is holy comic, setting them free to perform a uniquely valuable ministry."

While looking at the group conversing in just the right tones of silliness I asked, "What kind of ministry do they do, Grace?"

"They," Grace answered, "have dedicated themselves to minister to the laughter impaired, a rapidly growing group these days, sad to say. The ministers go about trying to teach those who make being human a habit to laugh at their guilt-ridden, greed-driven and fear-riddled selves, to follow the Ten Humor Commandments.

"I guarantee," Grace said, "if you follow the Commandments of Laughter you'll become a mystic fool, laughing all the way into life-after-life."

"What," I asked, "are the Ten Commandments of Humor?"

"Let me read them to you," Grace said, as she took a book out of a large brightly colored bag that sat comfortably on the seat next to her.

John Powers

"You shall keep holy every day by playing with God rather than playing at being God.

You shall honor all others by laughing at only what they give you permission to laugh at.

You shall take yourself lightly, but your chosen responsibilities in life seriously.

You shall use humor not only to survive the adversities of life but to thrive through them.

You shall shame no one with ridicule, mockery, or name-calling.

You shall laugh heartily at others' attempts at honest humor.

You shall use humor for only positive, healthy, and loving purposes, avoiding all ethnic or sexist jokes.

You shall share humorous stories and insights freely and generously.

You shall share anger appropriately with the right person, at the right time, and in the right way rather than using humor for harm's sake.

You shall preach and practice what you preach—eternal optimism and positive paranoia."

"A helpful list," I said. "Thank you, Grace. Let me ask, however, about an earlier comment you made about life-after-life. Did you mean to say that there is laughter in the afterlife?"

"Of course there is," Grace answered. "Heaven is a kinship of fools, clowns, and comics while hell is a committee that takes itself so seriously that it goes about making the possible impossible.

"You could say that laughter is heaven because it helps you accept, enjoy and share with others the reality of who you are, where you are at the moment. Eternal life, after all, is not an unending future but rather perpetual presence.

"Ultimately," Grace said, "there's as much laughter in your afterlife as you bring with you from your present life. You'll know, of course, that you're in heaven when you're once again happy to be yourself, glad to be with you, enjoying your own company.

"The problem for most people, however," Grace continued, "is not whether they believe in life-after-life but whether they can be at home with themselves on a rainy day no matter where they are. Everyone, of course, wants eternal life but very few are willing to die for the opportunity."

"What, Grace," I asked, while staring at the crowd of fools gathered around the altar, "are they discussing with such animation?"

"Their list of tips for a laughable life," Grace answered. "At least once a week someone in the group recommends a tip to be added to the list."

"How long is the list?" I asked.

"Not long," Grace said as she flipped forward a few pages in her book and began to read.

> "Listen to people who live on the
> edge, they know more about the
> center than do the higher-ups.
> Challenge all those who pretend to be
> perfect.
> Become fearlessly familiar with your
> inner family.
> Learn how to do subtraction. It will
> bring more happiness to your life
> than addition.
> Include the excluded.
> Reverence the imagination but not
> always the content of fantasy.
> Challenge all those who try to justify
> aggression to protect the name of
> an institution in the name of God.
> Repeat jokes even if you don't find them
> that funny anymore. Others might.

Don't let the anxious set your pace.

Cry as much as you like watching
commercials.

Listen as much to what others are not
saying as to what they are.

Remember that all religions are at best
understatements about God and
can never quite capture in dogma
the perpetual mystery that leaves
human beings trembling with fear.

Before offering up anything to God,
deal with it.

Listen to the music of nature.

Remain suspicious of bureaucracies.
They store ideas well but don't create them. People do.

Never walk by a playground without
trying a swing, slide or seesaw.

Don't beg God to change anything
just for you.

Optimism is learned. Choose it.

Be concerned more about the separation of Church and God than the
separation of Church and State.

Have breakfast with someone dangerous or different just to scramble
your ideas.

Work just as hard in old age to make
new friends as you do remembering
the friends you've made.
Give something away every day. That
way you won't have to worry about
taking it with you.

"That's the list as it stands now. However," Grace said as she smiled and pointed to a woman standing in the heart of the crowd, "a member of the group has suggested that the following proverb be added."

I was stunned with a feeling of familiarity when I casually turned to look at the woman who stood at the end of Grace's pointing finger.

"Fear less," Grace read, "hope more; eat less, chew more; whine less, breathe more; talk less, say more; hate less, love more, and all good things are yours."

I was so distracted by the beauty of the woman Grace had pointed out that not only didn't I pay much attention to the poem Grace was reciting but I wasn't even aware she'd finished, until that is, she tried to interrupt my reverie.

"So what do you think of the proverb, John? John!" Grace said, again trying to get my attention. Finally she said, "as in the before-life, so now, and, it seems, ever shall be, you still have trouble listening to me."

"What?" I asked as I climbed to my feet.

Realizing that she had no choice but to follow my distraction, Grace asked, "She looks familiar, doesn't she, John?"

"Yes," I answered. "Very! I feel like I've known her all my life and longer."

"Since you're not paying any attention to me why don't you go over and talk with her," Grace suggested.

"What's her name?" I asked as I began to walk toward the altar.

"Caitlin," Grace answered loudly enough for Caitlin to hear and respond with a turning of her head. "Caitlin, this is John," Grace said. "I believe you share the same birthday."

Within only a moment it felt like Caitlin and I had picked up the threads of a conversation we'd started weaving only yesterday. There were many years of stories to share but we took our time in the telling.

I began by telling the tale I've shared in this book, telling Caitlin how I'd been born on an island where the first and only commandment was, "Thou shall not be aware," how I'd met the beautiful Grace of God in life's most disturbing realities, in love and loss and how I'd found the gift of creativity hiding beneath the hurt.

Continuing to trust Caitlin with even more of my story, I spun the tale of my psychotherapy, telling her not only how a Master Artist of the Psyche had helped me face the powerfully influential inner family members of fear and grief but also how the Grace of a Higher Presence had helped me embrace failure, squeezing success out of its pain.

I finished weaving the tapestry of my story with the tale of a poor boy who'd not only pointed the way toward a kingdom called Kinship but also the way home to a self-honesty so deep that echoes of his laughter can still be heard.

Caitlin too had been born on Ignorance Island, in a place she called Florida. "It may have been a bright place," she said, "but it was not the kind of light that dispels the darkness. For that you need the light that only Grace can shine."

Caitlin went on weaving the tapestry of her story, telling me how she too had visited the Land of Pain, being, she cried, violently dragged by an abuser kicking and screaming over its borders. It had taken her a long time, she said, to learn to trust other people again, but by the Grace of God, she'd found a supportive group of men and women with a common story to tell.

For hours Caitlin and I sat in the front pew of the Temple sharing our comic, ironic, romantic, and tragic stories, laughing and crying as we remembered that ultimately we were victors not victims.

When we finally drifted into a moment of silence I looked over to see Grace patiently sitting in the back row of the Temple.

"I must confess, Caitlin," I whispered, "that although I've often ignored the presence of Grace in my life, the longer I know her the more I love and appreciate her."

Caitlin laughed as she turned to find Grace rising to her feet. "I have a feeling," Caitlin said, "that she's not finished with us yet, John, not by any stretch of the imagination."

"My friends," Grace said, as she walked down the Temple aisle toward the large Plexiglas podium that stood in the sanctuary, "God has given you all that God is so that you can do the same, so that you can add to the creativity, courage, compassion, contemplative spirit, and honest humor of life, so that you can face and embrace the ignorance, pain, fear, greed, grief, and violence that rage within and around you, so that you can be Gracebearers."

Just as Grace finished speaking every door in the Temple was suddenly thrown open. People, thousands of people, men and women came streaming into the worship hall, shaking hands, embracing, and kissing one another as they filled the Temple seats to overflowing.

I knew these people. I knew every one. They were my birthmates, my fellow students in classroom 90249. How many were left after forty-some-odd years of life I could not guess but I was thrilled to see every one.

Although I enthusiastically greeted dozens of brother and sister life-travelers as they poured into the empty places around Caitlin and I, I could not help but glance over toward Grace between the handshakes and embraces.

As I watched her stand proudly at the podium thumbing through her notes and papers one minute and the next smiling over the gathering crowd, I knew that the Grace of God would eternally travel in and through the universe making, strengthening, believing in, being present to, and enjoying life as it is and is meant to be.

I knew then that not only could you find the face of Grace in and between the lines of the universe's story but you could read it every day in and between the lines on every human face.

Grace, for me, is the face behind all others—my parents, brothers and sisters, especially Paul Joseph, Aquinas the Mentor as well as many other Passionate Monks, the Artist of Psyche, Richard the Missionary, Santos the Holy Child, and Caitlin, a birth-friend.

"May I have your attention please!" Grace announced as loudly as she could to be heard over the chatter. "We don't have a great deal of time for this mid-life class," she yelled, "so please come to order."

As silence filled the Temple Grace again spoke up. "This is a class for Gracebearers, for those willing to share the radiance of their own discoveries."

NOTES

[1]Joseph Campbell, *The Power of Myth*, (New York: Doubleday, 1988), p. xvi.

[2]Edward Sanford Martin, "My Name is Legion," *Masterpiece of Religious Verse*, edited by James Dalton Morrison, (New York: Harper and Row, 1948), p. 274.

[3]Statistical Data taken from Mihaly Csikszentmihalyi's *Flow; The Psychology of Optimal Experience*, (New York: Harper and Row, 1990), p. 29

[4]George Bernard Shaw, *St. Joan*, (Indianapolis: Bobbs Merill, 1975), pp. 68-69.

[5]Other versions of this story can be found in Scott Peck's, *The Different Drum*, (New York: Simon and Schuster, 1987), p. 224 and Anthony de Mello's, *The Song of the Bird*, (New York: Bantam Doubleday Dell Publishing Group Inc., 1984), p. 108-109.

[6]Paraphrased version of anonymous poem found on a hospital wall. Recorded in *Masterpieces of Religious Verse*, edited by James Dalton Morrison, (New York: Harper and Row, 1948), p. 435.

[7]Anthony Padavano, *Spiritual and Personal Development In Ministry*, an unpublished lecture, used with permission.

ABOUT THE AUTHOR

John D. Powers, CP, a Passionist priest, story-teller and author, is presently an associate retreat director at the Holy Family Monastery in West Hartford, Connecticut. He is the author of *Mirror, Mirror on the Wall; If They Could Speak;* and *Holy Human: Mystics for Our Time.* He is currently working on his next project for McCracken Press, *Spirations,* a book and two cassettes of monodramas inspired by the question, "If Citizens of the Bible could speak to us today, what might they say?"